Value-Added
Sales
Management

Value-Added Sales Management

A Guide for Salespeople and Their Managers

TOM REILLY

CONTEMPORARY
BOOKS

CHICAGO

Library of Congress Cataloging-in-Publication Data

Reilly, Thomas P.
    Value-added sales management : a guide for salespeople
and their managers / Tom Reilly.
        p.   cm.
    ISBN 0-8092-3787-3 (paper)
    1. Sales management.   2. Selling.   I. Title.
HF5438.4.R45   1993
658.8'1—dc20   92-43380
                                                                   CIP

Published by Contemporary Books, Inc.
180 North Michigan Avenue, Chicago, Illinois 60601
Manufactured in the United States of America
International Standard Book Number: 0-8092-3787-3

To my wife, Charlotte,
who for the past twenty-two years
has added more value to my life
than any one man deserves

Other books by Tom Reilly

Value-Added Selling Techniques: How to Sell More Profitably, Confidently, and Professionally
Selling Smart

Contents

Introduction

Congratulations! You're doing something that fewer than 10 percent of your peers will do this year . . . read a book on your profession. In my first book, *Value-Added Selling Techniques*, I shocked people with this statistic. Unfortunately, it's as true today as it was then. And fortunately, the same benefit that applied then applies now. As you read and use these ideas you're giving yourself the "Knowledge is Power" advantage.

I wrote my original book in response to salespeople's requests for help in dealing with price objections. Over five years, I tracked the number and kinds of objections salespeople brought to seminars. As you can imagine, price topped the list. It still does.

I've written this book in response to one of the most frequently asked questions I receive from sales managers, "Tom, how do we follow up on what you've taught us?" They recognize the fundamental truth of personal development and organizational change. All the sales training dollars in the world are meaningless unless management follows up.

Too often, companies spend incredible amounts of

money hiring the best people, give them the best training money can buy, arm them with amazing collateral support, and pay them well, but fail to give them the one thing that will make the difference: management attention and time. It reminds me of parents who spend enormous amounts of money raising their children but fail to give them time.

You build a value-added salesforce with consistent follow-up training by the first-line sales manager. To implement the ideas in this book successfully you must view training as the catalyst to change and management as the change agent. Sales managers looking for shortcuts are kidding themselves. Top-level management asking overnight results is unrealistic.

This book gives you insight into the value-added selling process, information on how to unleash the power of your salesforce, and substantive plans for execution. The need for value-added selling grows more urgent daily. As products become more similar, companies pledge to Total Quality Management, and consumers demand greater value, salespeople must rise to the occasion with value-added selling. Tough competitive selling is the game of the nineties and value-added selling is the price of admission. Are your salespeople prepared?

I've designed this book to help you achieve significant change. The first chapters offer a sales manager's perspective on value-added selling. Specifically, I'll walk you through the value-added selling process, offer statistical proof on what buyers really want, teach you to train your salespeople to sell value-added, offer ideas on how to handle price objections, sharpen your value-added negotiating skills, and challenge you to deliver value-added customer service.

The first chapters are for the salesperson in you, the later ones for the manager in you. I help you understand how organizations and people change and your role in the process. Since I'm asking you to be the change agent, you must understand the process inside out. You'll notice that I switch usage in this book between you and your salespeople. I do this because you are "selling managers" and it makes it easier to write and read.

I elaborate on the key dynamics for a sales management system. It reads like a menu for success. One dynamic is motivation. It's such a critical issue for sales managers that I've dedicated an entire chapter to the subject. Also, I've included a chapter on one of the most fascinating topics for sales managers: the plateaued salesperson.

I conclude with a kaleidoscope of interesting topics for managers. Things like managing in tough times, maximizing your distributor network, management and leader ship, and how marketing supports the value-added sales effort.

As I stated earlier, without your passionate commitment to follow-up training sessions the impact of outside training is minimal. To help you become an "in-house" trainer, I conclude with ideas for conducting your own sales training sessions.

By selling and managing the value-added way, you're giving yourself the competitive advantages of operating more profitably and focusing more strategically. Those who adopt this sales and management model experience the benefits of value-added selling. They lead instead of follow. Customers respect them. And their margins reflect their efforts. These benefits and more await you in the coming chapters. Read to understand. Practice to perfect. Apply to succeed.

Remember, it's the unique combination of your high level of initiative coupled with everyone else's apathy, indifference, and inertia that will make you successful.

Happy reading!

1
Introduction to Value-Added Selling

If you asked the average consumer to respond to the cue word "salesman," how would he or she respond? (Notice that I use the word *salesman* and not *salesperson*. This is not to discriminate against women: when you use the word *salesperson* it softens the response.) When I do this in seminars, salespeople respond with words like: liar, slick, pushy, mistrust, manipulative, high pressure, and then it gets worse!

These are salespeople telling me how they think consumers perceive our profession. This is particularly disturbing since this is *everything* I plan to do with my life. I'm proud of devoting my life to sales. Every time one of us sells something twenty-five American families benefit from it. As disturbing as this stereotype of salespeople is, there is a flip-side advantage.

I have a theory that buyers have a collage of faces on the wall directly across their desks. On this collage are the faces of all the salespeople they know. When you call on buyers, you either blend in with the collage or stand out. If you use the same tired routine that every salesperson brings to the table, buyers treat you like every other sales-person.

On the other hand, if you bring to the table something creative, innovative, and solution-oriented, your face jumps out in 3-D fashion. If you bring a value-added package to the table, the buyer treats you uniquely. In spite of the negative biases consumers hold toward salespeople, you can use it to your advantage to differentiate yourself from the crowd. This is the message you must take to your salespeople.

The essence of value-added selling is differentiating yourself and your package within a customer-oriented environment. Buying and selling is an information exchange. The buyer gives you a certain amount of information, you process it and feed back more information to him. The degree of overlap between the information he gives you and what you feed back determines the likelihood of your doing business (see Figure 1).

FIGURE 1
INFORMATION EXCHANGE

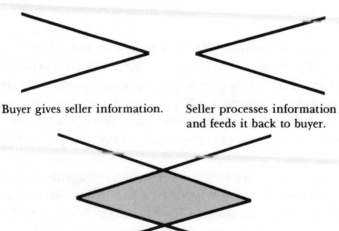

Buyer gives seller information.   Seller processes information and feeds it back to buyer.

Overlap equals congruence of information.

In traditional selling, the salesperson "firehoses" the buyer with product information and technitrivia before giving him an opportunity to explain his needs. There's no exchange. It's one-way communication and the salesperson does all the talking. Imagine the impact this has on the buyer! He perceives the salesperson as a "me-oriented, product-driven, I'm-going-to-sell-something" individual.

Conversely, buyers perceive the value-added salesperson as interested in the buyer. Value-added salespeople are honest, customer-oriented, and proactive. They have a strong concern for people and results. That's what this book is about—how you create the value-added sales organization.

WHAT IS VALUE?

Before defining value-added selling, we must define value. We could use complex economic jargon, but for salespeople value is simple. It's three things. I call these the three Ps: personal, perception, and performance.

First, value is a very *personal* thing. Like fingerprints, everyone has his own definition. To some, it's quality. To others, it's service. And to others, it's technical support. And yes, there are some who define it as price.

Last year I spoke to a health-care industry association. Before my presentation, a panel of hospital presidents discussed industry trends. The audience was manufacturers of health-care related items. The panel members were their customers. One panel member boldly stated, "As far as I'm concerned all this value-added stuff you guys talk about is trivial."

The air was thick with animosity. The audience recoiled at his impertinence. And I thought to myself, "This is great. I'm supposed to give them ninety minutes on value-added selling and one of their customers just said it's trivial!"

He finished with, "The reason I say this is that every one of you will call on me tomorrow and dictate to me your notion of value-added. Yet, not a one of you will ask me how I define value-added." He paused, and the group slowly nodded their acceptance. I breathed a sigh of relief. He laid the perfect foundation for my talk.

Value is a personal concept. Each person defines it in his own unique way. I've always believed this, and this experience reinforced my convictions. For your salespeople to sell value, they must first define it in customer terms. Why would anyone pay more to do business with one company over another? Why should your customer pay more to do business with you?

Second, value is also a *perception*. You've heard the old saying, "Seeing is believing"? Well, perceiving is believing. It's ultimately the customer's perception that counts. Perception addresses cosmetic and stylistic issues. Image plays an important role in reassuring buyers that they are making the correct buying decision.

Please understand that style and image are cosmetic but not superficial. When buyers evaluate two packages, one generic and the other a well-known brand name, the buyer reacts differently to the brand name. Packaging plays to perception.

In my seminars, I demonstrate this to the audience. I present them with two boxes. One is tattered and contains a moderately priced, new ballpoint pen. The other is a new package. It reads "Cross™, 10 kt. gold-filled, model 4502." When I remove it from the cardboard sleeve, I point out the leatherette box with brass trim and a hinge. I ask the group, "Which would you prefer?" They unanimously choose the Cross Pen.* When I ask why, they respond that

---

*Cross Pen is a registered trademark of the Cross Pen Company of Lincoln, Rhode Island.

it looks better and has a brand name. Perception. They decide on perception. Packaging influences their decision. Imagine how they feel when I open the box and remove an inexpensive plastic pen. It's the same functionally but has less perceived value.

A book buyer at one of the major chains reviewed my first book and told us to redesign the cover. When I pursued the issue, he responded with, "Because buyers judge books by their covers." We redesigned the cover!

Here's a caveat to live by: You may get the business by creating the perception of greater value, but you keep it through the performance of greater value. This is our third P: *performance.*

What perception is to style, performance is to substance. Your package must have substance to satisfy customer needs. Perception makes the buyer feel better about buying your product while performance makes him feel better about owning your product. Customer satisfaction is a function of your performance relative to the customer's expectations. If you outperform expectations, you have satisfied customers. If you underperform expectations, you have dissatisfied customers. It's OK to promise a lot if you always deliver more than you promise.

Style and substance work hand in glove to achieve maximum selling advantage. Refer to the matrix in Figure 2. Quadrant one is the ideal scenario. You have plenty of perceived value (style) and plenty of performance value (substance). In quadrant two, you have no style but plenty of substance. A tough sale on the front end. In quadrant three, you have plenty of style with nothing to back it up— a sure way to lose the business in the long run. Quadrant four is the least desirable: no style and no substance. Good luck!

Your salespeople must understand that selling value-added is predicated on their defining value in customer terms, reinforcing customer perceptions that you are the value-added supplier, and exceeding customer expectations.

FIGURE 2
STYLE AND SUBSTANCE

STYLE

		Yes	No
SUBSTANCE	Yes	1 You have maximum advantage.	2 A tough sale to make, but you'll probably keep the business.
	No	3 You'll have an easier time selling it, but you'll struggle with repeat business.	4 Good luck!

WHAT IS "VALUE-ADDED"?

In my research, I discovered the first reference to value-added circa 1916. It related to manufacturing and the source was the U.S. government. Today the Department of Commerce defines value-added as the "difference between raw material input and finished product output." In simple terms, it's everything your company does to the product from start to finish. And finish includes postsale treatments.

There are two types of value-added: qualitative and quantitative. *Qualitative* value-added is more subjective and addresses perceptual issues. Some refer to it as "soft" value. This includes how long your company has been in business, your reputation, brand name recognition, and your company's position in the market. All are important for reassuring the customer emotionally that you're the best solution.

Quantitative value-added is objective and measurable. Some refer to it as "hard" value: the financial impact your solution has on the customer. It's efficiency, productivity, and effectiveness. Quantitative value-added is logical reassurance for your prospect.

Every product has intrinsic value for the customer. This is what goes into your product to make it good. Some of it the customer needs and wants. Other parts of it the customer may not want. To sell intrinsic value means your salespeople are selling what you deem important. In a market-driven business, customers define value-added for you. In a production-driven business, companies dictate value-added to the customers and spend time and money arguing customers into submission.

THE VALUE-ADDED SELLING PHILOSOPHY

Value-added selling is a philosophy of doing business. It's proactively looking for ways to enhance, augment, or enlarge your bundled package for the customer.

Value-added selling must be a philosophy. It's a passion, attitude, or mindset toward doing business. It's not a cliché, an annual theme, or a sales training course. It transcends a knee-jerk reaction to a price-sensitive market. It's permanent, not faddish. It's a simple belief system of going the extra mile all the time.

Proactive. It's everything you do before price becomes an issue. Being proactive means initiating, preempting, and anticipating. Proactively selling value-added is "never having to say you're sorry" when it comes to price. The concept is sound. Invest substantial value on the front end so that price becomes less of an issue on the back end.

When the customer buys, he gets three things: the

product, the supplier, and the salesperson. This is the bundled package concept. The salesperson is an important part of the package. Research from two Fortune 100 companies indicates that the salesperson contributes between 35 and 37 percent of the value that customers receive. At most, the product and company are each one-third. The salesperson is *at least* one-third the value that the customer receives!

This concept intimidates some salespeople, while others find it exciting. It means that the same product from the same company sold by one salesperson is substantially different from the same product from the same company sold by another salesperson. The buyer purchases a bundle of value, not just the product. The salesperson is a viable part of the bundle.

When salespeople tell me that their products and companies are no better or worse than the competition, I ask if they personally are worth anything to the customer. They hesitate before responding to that question.

Train your salespeople to sell value-added by helping them redefine and understand what they're selling. Teach them that value, like beauty, is in the eye of the beholder. Encourage them to be proactive.

There are five conditions under which value-added selling happens. You can review any piece of business your company lost because of price and determine which of these was missing. First, you must arrive early in the decision process. When you penetrate early, you have an opportunity to sell the prospect on the concept of value-added. You can help write specifications unique to your product. If you arrive too late in the process, it is more of a price and product decision.

Second, focus long-term. Value-added is not a short-term concept: it typically involves ideas whose time must come. To experience the scope of benefits the buyer must own the product for a while. Much of the value-added comes after acquisition. The buyer must own and use the product to take full advantage of the bundled-package solution. Selling value-added is like painting a beautiful portrait. You do it a brush stroke at a time. Every little brush stroke, by itself, does not mean much. It's the combination of brush strokes that form a beautiful portrait. And many of these come after the buyer becomes a customer—long-term benefits.

Price shoppers make short-term decisions. Value-added shoppers make long-term decisions. Changing the way your prospect views the sale paves the way for value-oriented decisions. Educate your prospect on the benefits of thinking and planning long-term.

Third, penetrate the account at the highest levels. Top management makes conceptual decisions. Lower-level employees make product-oriented decisions that typically involve price. High-level management uses a different time horizon. They're concerned with longer-term issues: a predicate for value-added selling.

Fourth, penetrate the account deep. Involve as many people as you can. Create pull for your solution. Develop an internal salesforce that sells for you when you're not there. Teach your salespeople to burrow their way through accounts developing strong relationships and alliances. Everyone brings a different agenda to the table. The more priorities you get on the table the less important price becomes.

Fifth, define value in customer terms. Customers are not interested in how you define value. They prefer their definition so you can mold your solution to fit their needs. The Japanese criticize American industry because it focuses on the intrinsic quality of products versus the customers' definition of quality. I call this "application" quality. It's egocentric to pressure buyers into your definition of value.

Selling value-added is teaching buyers to make prudent buying decisions, to think long-term, to consider all organizational goals, and to focus off product and on the total solution.

WHY SELL VALUE-ADDED?

Over half of the companies with whom I work are the least expensive in their industry. Their salespeople attend seminars craving information on how to compete with organizations that offer higher quality, better service, and greater support. They say, "Tom, our only advantage is a cheaper price. And with the stroke of a pen another company can undercut us!" These salespeople recognize the inherent flaw of using price as the primary weapon. There is always someone out there who can sell it a little cheaper. Indirectly, you tell customers that if they can buy it cheaper go ahead. After all, you've been selling price all along.

Customers Want Value

Fewer than one in six is a true price shopper. Research indicates that the actual number hovers around 16 percent. Even though price tops the list of objections salespeople bring to seminars, most concede that true price shoppers represent a small percentage of their customer base. A *true* price shopper considers price only. For others, price is *a* decision variable—not *the* decision variable.

If you're curious about the percentage of true price shoppers in your market, use this informal rule of thumb. What market share does the least expensive alternative in your market own? This represents the percent of price-only decisions made in your industry.

So what do buyers want? Current studies report that consumers prefer quality over price. The actual percentage varies by industry, but the vast majority rank quality as more important. The concern for quality in the United

Value-added selling is also a wonderful defensive selling strategy because it helps nail shut the back door. It lowers your customer attrition rate. And research indicates that a 2 percent reduction in attrition rate has the same effect on profitability as a 10 percent cost-reduction campaign. Satisfied customers are loyal customers. They're also fantastic advertising. Word of mouth is the most potent form of marketing. Nothing smacks of credibility more than unsolicited positive remarks about a company.

Last year 67 percent of my business came from referrals. My second greatest pull came from people reading my book. Third, my articles appearing in national publications pulled business. And fourth, paid advertising. Please understand that I believe in paid advertising. It works! The point is that loyal, satisfied customers not only come back, they bring their friends.

The Impact of a "Price-Only" Strategy

What are the implications of a price-only selling strategy? You must sell more to compensate for the lost profitability. If your company has the potential for selling at a 40 percent gross margin and you discount by 10 percent to buy the business, you must increase unit sales by 33 percent to compensate for the lost profitability. If you discount by 20 percent, you must double your unit sales to earn the same profit. A 30 percent discount requires a whopping 400 percent increase to compensate for the lost profit.

Ask yourself this question: "Can we quadruple our sales with existing resources or must we invest more to expand our facilities?" Making it up in volume is not always the correct prescription. One school of thought proposes that "if it's not a good deal for us at a lower margin, why do we want even more of that business?" Is more volume at less profit good for your company? Or, would it make sense to let the competition have it? You

States has grown from 30 to 80 percent since 1978. Our research indicates that during tough economic times quality leaders thrive as customers become more discriminating with their purchasing dollars. They want "better" for their money.

Customers also want service. The White House Office on Consumers' Affairs was so concerned about the condition of business in this country that it commissioned a study to determine why people stop doing business with a company. They discovered that 68 percent quit because of vendor indifference—not price! People want service. They want quality. They want to get as good as they give.

Customer perceptions of equity are the chief cause of price objections. Many times it's not the *price* people object to, it's the *package* for the price. In *The Wealth of Nations*, Adam Smith wrote, "The real price of everything, what everything really costs to the man who wants to acquire it, is the toil and trouble of acquiring it." This is the equitable exchange of commodities—the buyer's time and money for your product. Buyers say, "If your product has greater perceived and performance value to me than my commodities, I'll gladly exchange one for the other."

Buyers want fair treatment. They want quality. They want service. They want people who genuinely care. And, they want a fair price.

It's Good for Business

Research demonstrates that companies who wield service as their primary competitive weapon can charge about 10 percent more for their goods and services and outgrow their competition. Redefining your "package" to include value-added services is a great way to boost profitability and increase account retention.

It costs the average company six times more money to get a new customer than to keep an existing one happy.

comes after acquisition. The buyer must own and use the product to take full advantage of the bundled-package solution. Selling value-added is like painting a beautiful portrait. You do it a brush stroke at a time. Every little brush stroke, by itself, does not mean much. It's the combination of brush strokes that form a beautiful portrait. And many of these come after the buyer becomes a customer—long-term benefits.

Price shoppers make short-term decisions. Value-added shoppers make long-term decisions. Changing the way your prospect views the sale paves the way for value-oriented decisions. Educate your prospect on the benefits of thinking and planning long-term.

Third, penetrate the account at the highest levels. Top management makes conceptual decisions. Lower-level employees make product-oriented decisions that typically involve price. High-level management uses a different time horizon. They're concerned with longer-term issues: a predicate for value-added selling.

Fourth, penetrate the account deep. Involve as many people as you can. Create pull for your solution. Develop an internal salesforce that sells for you when you're not there. Teach your salespeople to burrow their way through accounts developing strong relationships and alliances. Everyone brings a different agenda to the table. The more priorities you get on the table the less important price becomes.

Fifth, define value in customer terms. Customers are not interested in how you define value. They prefer their definition so you can mold your solution to fit their needs. The Japanese criticize American industry because it focuses on the intrinsic quality of products versus the customers' definition of quality. I call this "application" quality. It's egocentric to pressure buyers into your definition of value.

Selling value-added is teaching buyers to make prudent buying decisions, to think long-term, to consider all organizational goals, and to focus off product and on the total solution.

WHY SELL VALUE-ADDED?

Over half of the companies with whom I work are the least expensive in their industry. Their salespeople attend seminars craving information on how to compete with organizations that offer higher quality, better service, and greater support. They say, "Tom, our only advantage is a cheaper price. And with the stroke of a pen another company can undercut us!" These salespeople recognize the inherent flaw of using price as the primary weapon. There is always someone out there who can sell it a little cheaper. Indirectly, you tell customers that if they can buy it cheaper go ahead. After all, you've been selling price all along.

Customers Want Value

Fewer than one in six is a true price shopper. Research indicates that the actual number hovers around 16 percent. Even though price tops the list of objections salespeople bring to seminars, most concede that true price shoppers represent a small percentage of their customer base. A *true* price shopper considers price only. For others, price is *a* decision variable—not *the* decision variable.

If you're curious about the percentage of true price shoppers in your market, use this informal rule of thumb. What market share does the least expensive alternative in your market own? This represents the percent of price-only decisions made in your industry.

So what do buyers want? Current studies report that consumers prefer quality over price. The actual percentage varies by industry, but the vast majority rank quality as more important. The concern for quality in the United want your competition to get some of that low-margin, high-aggravation business. Have you ever taken a piece of business and resented it afterward?

Peter Drucker says that "the mark of a good manager is knowing which projects to work on. But, the mark of a great manager is knowing which projects *not* to work on." As a sales manager you can extrapolate and say, "the mark of a good salesperson is knowing which accounts to pursue. But, the mark of a great salesperson is knowing which accounts *not* to pursue."

Here is a sampling of the answers I receive from salespeople when I ask, "What is the impact of cutting your price?"

- "You must sell more to compensate for it."
- "It damages the customer's trust bond with you. Your credibility is diminished."
- "It sets an irreversible precedent. No one pays sticker price for a new car."
- "It destroys brand loyalty."
- "It's demotivating to the salesforce."
- "You start a bigger price war."

Common sense dictates that when you earn less money on a sale something must give: service, quality of raw materials, follow-up after the sale, etc. Therefore, the customer also loses. At times, discounting is a good business decision. There are times when you want a piece of business for nonprofit reasons. Discounting must be strategic, not accidental.

Value-added selling is good for the customer because he wants and needs it. It's good for your company because of the higher profit margins. It's also good for your salespeople. Those who sell value-added work from positions of high self-esteem because they feel like an integral part of the package. They recognize and accept their value to the customer. Most people want to feel needed and valuable to someone else. Job satisfaction is higher for value-added salespeople because they're involved and committed to customer satisfaction. When they perform their job the way it's designed, it's a triple win—for the customer, the company, and the salesperson.

Abraham Maslow wrote fifty years ago that people have a burning passion to be better today than yesterday and better tomorrow than today. He called this self-actualization: becoming all that you can become. Value-added selling is the perfect fit for this philosophy of doing and being the most you can.

Why Don't Salespeople Sell Value-Added?

If all this about value-added selling is true, why don't more salespeople do it? There are four reasons. First, it's easy to sell price. Selling value-added is time-consuming and challenging. How much effort does it require to ask, "What price gets your business?"

Second, the salesperson lacks something. He may lack the knowledge or understanding that this is important to his organization. He may lack skills because his company has never invested in training. He may lack the conviction that his company is worth the price difference. Over half of the people I train are unable to answer this question spontaneously in a seminar: "Why should I pay more to do business with your company?" They just don't know.

Third, fear. They fear being perceived as gouging the customer. Guilt plays a role. If another customer gets a better price, the salesperson knows it and feels uneasy not giving everyone the same deal. Fear also applies to losing the business: "If I charge too much I may lose the account." That's true. If you charge too much, it could come back to haunt you; and if you charge too little, it could come back to haunt the customer.

Fourth, and more common than many care to admit,

is projection. This is attributing or "projecting" your feelings onto other people. If the salesperson is a price shopper in her own life, she will get more price objections than others on the staff. She shops price and assumes everyone does. She leads with price and creates her own objections. "Mr. Buyer, when you make your final decision, price will be an issue, won't it?" She returns to the office and tells her boss that she received (created) a price objection. I wager that the salesperson on your staff who screams most about your price is also a price shopper in her own life.

What do you do about these salespeople? Educate them. Teach them about the importance of profitability to your company's future. Train them on your value-added philosophy and give them the skills to sell it. That's probably why you're reading this book. Alleviate their fears about losing business if they sell value and not price. And convince your price-shopper salespeople that not everyone is looking for the cheapest price—fewer than one in six is truly a price shopper.

CHAPTER SUMMARY

This chapter introduced you to the concept of value-added selling. At this point, you understand the philosophy and how it applies to your business. You have some great arguments to convert your salespeople to this sales attitude. In the next few chapters, you will learn some very specific ways to turn your salesforce into a team of value-added selling professionals. It's a great time for you and your company to initiate these ideas. Give your salesforce the value-added advantage. Lead them in the challenge.

2
Proactive Selling Strategies

When is the best time to handle a price objection? When it's raised? Later? Never? How about *before* it becomes an issue? This is proactive selling. It's preempting the price objection by adding enough value to the package so that price is less important. Proactive salespeople are order makers. Reactive salespeople are order takers. Reactive salespeople are like vending machines that only dispense products. Proactive salespeople take the initiative with a value-added solution.

There is an inverse relationship between the amount of time you spend on the front end of the sale versus the amount of time you spend on the back end resurrecting a dead sale. The more time you invest analyzing customer needs, studying, and designing customized solutions, and presenting relevant value-added solutions, the less time you spend handling price objections.

In this chapter, I focus on how your salespeople can proactively sell value-added to avoid the full brunt of price resistance. Much of this chapter focuses on "capture," that is, pursuing new business. These same ideas can be used with existing customers.

The value-added selling process begins with preparation and ends with support strategies. It is *not* a sequential strategy. Sequential strategies dictate that you rigidly adhere to a structured flow of events.

These proactive strategies are more dynamic. Certainly preparation precedes calling, and the needs analysis precedes a feature-benefit presentation. But continuous probing, presenting, and supporting occur throughout the process. For example, in-depth questioning plays a major role on the front end to identify customer needs. On the back end, it plays a major role in discovering new opportunities. I call this "opportunity probing." Remember, even though I present these in a logical order, the process evolves into a sale, which evolves into another sale, and so on.

This chapter focuses on different value-added selling strategies. The next chapter focuses on how these strategies fit into a value-added buying model, the customer's Critical Buying Path.™ The salesperson's role changes over time, and effective salespeople adapt to the changing sales environment. By teaching your salespeople how to use the correct skill at the right moment, you're helping them to engineer a value-added buying decision that creates a win-win situation for your company and the customer. By the time you finish this chapter, you will have made enough notes and generated enough ideas to begin preparing your salesforce to sell value-added.

PREPARATION

Knowledge is Power! How often have you heard this? There is a scene in the movie *Patton* when George C. Scott, who plays Patton, stands on the hillside overlooking his forces battling the German army and says, "Rommel, you magnificent bastard, I read your book!" He then goes on to defeat Rommel's army.

The first way your salespeople deliver value is with

knowledge. As your salespeople study, they build their intellectual capital and increase their value to the customer. Professional study brings substantial return on your time investment.

Strategic Value Analysis

The first step in professional study is to perform a strategic value analysis. This focuses on three areas: the market, competition, and company. Answer these questions in a group setting with your salespeople to discover what they know and don't know. Knowing which questions to ask is as important as knowing the answers.

The Market

What are the three most important trends in our industry?

How has our industry changed over the past five years?

Where is it going in the next five years?

How many market segments do we have and what are they?

What are our greatest potential growth areas this year and next?

What outside forces are applying pressure to our industry?

Which mode is our industry in (growth, maturity, decline)?

Which of our customers are doing well (poorly)?

The Competition

Who are our top three competitors?

What are their strengths?

In what ways are they vulnerable?

How can we attack their weaknesses?

How do they compare along these dimensions: quality, service, and price?

The Company

In what ways are we truly unique?

In what ways are we vulnerable?

Do customers view us as production-driven or market-driven?

Why do we lose existing customers?

Why do we lose prospective business?

Why do we sometimes gain a piece of business in spite of our higher price?

What are the three most common objections we hear from our customers?

Where does the greatest part of our value exist—in the product, the company, or the salesforce?

A fourth important area to ask questions is customers. I cover this in the section on analyzing customer needs.

VIP List

Once you have performed your strategic value analysis, have your salespeople construct a VIP list—Value In Purchasing. This is a list of value-added extras your company offers. Use these tips for the VIP list:

1. Have the group name at least twenty value-added extras your company offers. This includes product value-added, company value-added, and salesperson value-added.
2. Once you've compiled the list, dress it up. Use your laser printer or have your printer typeset it and put it on high-quality stock.
3. Make this part of your sales and marketing strategy. Your salespeople can use it many ways:
   - During call preparation, to determine which value-added extras to discuss on the call
   - As a positioning tool on a sales call

- As a page in a proposal
- As a tool for handling price objections
- By faxing a copy to the buyer the day before a final decision

Your imagination is the only thing that limits you. It's amazing how many uses your salespeople can discover for this list. You'll notice a high level of enthusiasm by salespeople when you perform this exercise. You're focusing them on hope and possibility. You're reminding them of all the reasons your company is a great value for the customer. It's exciting as you feel their motivation grow. You'll know that you're creating a value-added salesforce.

Jumbo CDs

Fewer than 10 percent of the salespeople I train have a systematic way for allocating their sales time. This is a great opportunity. If no one else does it and you do, you have a tremendous advantage over your competition. You don't have to be incredibly smart to beat your competition, just a little smarter than them. This means strategically investing your sales time in those areas where you know that you get the greatest return on time invested.

What would you do if someone died tomorrow and left you one hundred thousand dollars with the following provision? You have three investment options from which to choose: First, put the money in a passbook savings account. This normally draws about 4 to 5 percent interest. Option number two is to put the money in a CD that pays a few points over passbook rates. Option number three is a Jumbo CD. At the hundred-thousand-dollar level you qualify for a Jumbo CD, which pays a higher rate than the CD. Which would you do?

When I ask this question in seminars, I hear a unanimous "Jumbo CD." When I ask why, the people point to the greater return. It's ironic that they know how to invest their money, a replaceable commodity, but don't invest their time as prudently. Time is more than money—it's life!

Teach your salespeople to focus their sales efforts with a laserlike intensity on the types of customers who buy value-added. These are Jumbo CDs, and the following three questions help you identify them.

• *Who are your six "best" accounts?* "Best" is arbitrary. It means anything you want it to mean. It could mean volume, profitability, ease of doing business, quick pay, etc. I suggest that you weigh these variables any way you like. Maybe half profit and half volume.

• *What three things do your "best" customers have in common?* Is it their size, location, marketplace, S.I.C., product quality, market position, number of employees, or any other variable? The more common denominators you discover the more specific the profile. Look for variables that are objective and measurable.

• *Who else shares these common denominators?* For some reason your company, products, and salespeople appeal to a certain type of customer. You don't need to get Freudian and ask *why*, you only need to ask *who*. These are your Jumbo CD prospects. This is where you allocate your sales and marketing resources. The return on investment is much higher with Jumbos.

Just because you encourage your salespeople to invest in Jumbo CDs doesn't mean they should be ignoring other prospects. Everyone deserves the courtesy of being treated with the value-added mentality, but not every account deserves the intensity of a value-added sales campaign. While your competition randomly assigns account priority, teach your salespeople to think, plan, and sell strategically. In addition to making them better salespeople, it makes them better businesspeople.

You've prepared your salespeople by building their knowledge base while increasing their worth to the customer. You've built their confidence by clarifying the total value your company offers. You've focused them with a Jumbo CD guidance system. Now you're ready for them to go into the field and begin the value-added sale.

THE CUSTOMER AUDIT

You go to the doctor's office for a flu shot. He greets you with, "Tom, I'm glad you're here today. We have a brand new form of insulin. It's an oral medication, which means you don't have to jab yourself in the arm twice each day. Because of its special time-release element you only need to take this medicine once a week instead of fourteen times per week. And the actual usage cost of this insulin is about one-half the cost of traditional insulin. What do you think?"

"That's great, Doc. But I don't have diabetes! I'm here for a flu shot!"

The doctor prescribed without diagnosing the problem. Lawyers have a name for this: malpractice. This is an occupational hazard for salespeople. In sales, we call it the "firehose" approach. Salespeople call on buyers and blast them with thirty minutes of features and benefits. This is a product-driven approach to sales.

Performing a customer audit is the single most important thing salespeople can do. The customer audit is selling from the inside out. You're selling as if you're really the customer's business partner. The customer audit is viewing life from the customer's perspective. To do this you must perform a thorough needs analysis.

The needs analysis is a systematic fact-finding mission. Asking questions is important for several reasons. First, you must fully understand the customer's needs. How can you sell value-added if you don't know how the customer defines it? Do you remember the five conditions under which value-added selling happens? One of these is defining value-added in customer terms.

Second, it's important for the customer to understand that his needs go beyond the generic. Customers make value-added buying decisions when they understand and accept that they have enhanced needs. The first sale your salespeople make is that the buyer's needs transcend the generic. I call the buyer's *objective needs awareness* a "constructive pain level." People change when they feel the "pain" or "tension" of the status quo's failure to meet their evolving and emerging needs.

Third, a spin-off benefit of the needs analysis is that involvement lowers resistance to change. When people are actively involved in the change process, they are less resistant. Buyers involved in the sale are less resistant to new ideas and more committed to action. The greater the involvement, the greater the commitment.

Fourth, the value-added salesperson is an educator. He educates customers to make better value-oriented buying decisions. And he educates the way Socrates did—with questions. By strategically asking the right questions at the right moment, he creates buyer objective needs awareness. The questions guide the buyer through a better decision path. The salesperson enlarges the buyer's understanding of his needs and shifts the focus to long-term ownership issues versus short-term acquisition costs.

Performing the needs analysis, creating an objective needs awareness, and maximizing buyer involvement produce the internal buyer motivation to *want* to change. When your salespeople generate enthusiasm for a solution, the buyer is more anxious to buy than you are to sell. Closing is simply working out the details.

In the needs analysis, teach your salespeople to begin with an understanding of the customer's needs, wants, and desires for a product, vendor, and salesperson. Help your salespeople understand the driving forces behind these needs. It's important to begin with the customer's expectations on the table.

From there, ask how the customer is attempting to meet these needs. These are performance-oriented questions. They expose the gap that exists between *what he needs* and *what he's using*. This seed of dissatisfaction grows into a powerful change motivator as the salesperson carefully and skillfully probes. Remember what I said earlier about customer satisfaction. It's outperforming expectations. If you "help" the buyer discover that his current way of attempting to meet his needs fails to meet his expectations, customer dissatisfaction sets in. This is your foot in the door.

Probing Tips

Ask 80 percent open-ended questions. Open-ended questions encourage customers to elaborate freely. They elicit more information. Open questions involve buyers and lower the resistance to change. Closed questions limit the other person to short answers. They raise buyer antagonism because he feels interrogated and not interviewed.

Ask about the customer's greatest purchasing fear. If your salespeople identify the customer's greatest purchasing fear and alleviate it, they build commitment for your option.

Ask what his customers desire from him. What the buyer's customers want from him signals what he wants from your company. If your buyer is in a quality-oriented market, that's what he wants from you. If service sells in his market, sell service. And if he's in a price-sensitive industry, expect price resistance.

Focus on how the customer is vulnerable in his market. Determining buyer vulnerabilities helps your salespeople design their sales strategy. If your package offers the prospect a way to reduce his vulnerability, you have given him a value-added solution.

Avoid begging for price objections. Salespeople unwittingly beg for price objections by asking if price is an issue. It's always important if you ask! If the budget issue surfaces ask, "What *range* are we working with?" Range implies flexibility and suggests that the buyer has latitude.

Probe for long-term issues. A long-term focus is crucial to value-added selling. Many times, buyers get so preoccupied with short-term acquisition cost that your salespeople must refocus them. Teach your salespeople to be master interviewers. Work on probing skills twice as much as closing skills. The more time they spend probing the less time needed to close.

Pressure Points

Look for buyer pressure points. A pressure point is any condition that induces the buyer to pay more to do business with you. The more of these your salespeople identify in the probing phase, the greater your confidence in "holding the line" on pricing. Train your salespeople to watch for pressure points. This list will help.

- Timing/scheduling—a sense of urgency
- The vendor's limited-inventory situation—i.e., the goods could be sold elsewhere more profitably
- Many customers competing for the vendor's attention
- The customer's specialized need
- The vendor's unique application
- The buyer's budget or funding source—i.e., co-op
- A brand bias
- Credit status
- Bad experience with competition

- Compliance (government regulations, association standards, peer pressure)
- Buying American
- Budget deadlines—money that must be spent or it is lost
- Location
- Being cheap has an impact on their image

Twenty-Five Important Questions

The following list of questions will help your salespeople become master interviewers. Since this is a generic list, you may want to add some industry-specific questions to your list. Encourage your salespeople to use this list. Have them place a copy in each account file. Over time, they need to ask and answer these to build a value-added sales climate.

1. Tell me about your marketplace.
2. What trends do you see in your market?
3. Where is your industry headed?
4. Who are your customers?
5. What do your customers look for when they come to you?
6. How does your decision process work?
7. How long has your company been in this market?
8. Who is your competition?
9. What advantages do you have over them?
10. In what ways are you vulnerable to them?
11. How long have you been with the company?
12. How does this decision affect you personally?
13. What are you looking for in a supplier?
14. What kind of technical support do you need on this project?
15. What delivery and availability does your project require?
16. Tell me about the product specifications needed to meet your standards.

17. How do you currently handle your needs?
18. Who is your current supplier?
19. How well has your current supplier met your needs?
20. What type of feedback have you received from your people who are using this?
21. If you could change anything about your current supplier, what would you change?
22. What would be your idea of the ideal product?
23. What would you like to see us do for you that your current supplier is not doing?
24. If you were a supplier, what would you do differently?
25. If you could improve something about the service level you're receiving currently, what would you change and how would that help your business?

Customer Critical Path

Every customer has a critical path for buying and using your product. This goes beyond the typical decision-making process. It begins with the moment a need exists and continues through the time when the customer is using, reordering, and disposing of your package. The path differs for each buyer but each has three main stages: planning, acquisition, and usage. The more accurately your salespeople identify the buyer's steps the greater the likelihood he can position value-added along the path.

This is a great tool for understanding the customer's needs and for brainstorming on how to deliver more value-added. In the next chapter, I detail the Critical Buying Path model and how the salesperson's role changes vis-à-vis this model. It's important that your salesforce think about this during the needs analysis stage.

Your group has invested heavily in gathering information. Now they must give information to convince the buyer of your value-added solution.

PERSUASION AND INFORMATION SHARING

The sale is an information exchange. You gather a certain amount of information and share a certain amount of information. The degree of overlap between the two determines the likelihood of your getting the business. The first part of this chapter focused on the customer audit: gathering information about customer needs. This part of the chapter helps your salespeople give enough relevant information to raise the buyer desire to the boiling point.

Presentation Ideas

These ideas can be used anytime throughout the sales process. They enhance your presentation. I encourage you to work with your salespeople to help them develop these presentation skills.

Watch your wording. Too often, salespeople beg for price objections with their wording. They say things such as, "our *list* price," which telegraphs that there is some maneuvering room. *"Your* price" indicates that everyone pays a different price. *"Normally* what we get for this is . . . " also creates a mindset of flexibility about price. Teach your salespeople to select their wording very carefully. Simply use, "The price is. . . . " This signals that everyone pays the same for the product.

Sandwich and summarize. When presenting the price, recap your benefits and sandwich the price between them. "Mr. Buyer, for everything we discussed: the shorter lead time, improved product quality, and technical support, the price is ——, and this includes the entire bundle of value you liked about our solution." This casts price in a different light. You're reminding the buyer that the package transcends the price issue.

Sell long-term. Price shoppers are short-term thinkers.

They are concerned with the present. Their perspective is the acquisition cost that appears on the invoice versus the long-term cost of owning and using the product. When your salespeople refocus the buyer long-term, they spotlight the postsale value-added your company offers. Teach your salespeople to ask questions about the customer's long- and short-term buying objectives. Then, have them support the long-term concept by presenting to it.

Sell conceptually. Conceptual selling is a special challenge. It's selling ideas not products. Conceptual selling involves big-picture issues like customer satisfaction, cash flow, competitive advantage, improved morale, redeployment of resources, and image enhancement. You're broadening the buyer's perspective. When you sell conceptually, you sell the solution not the package, the application not the box, or the results not the means. Price is less important in a conceptual sale. These decisions are made higher in the organization and typically involve a long-term perspective. If you tap into this mindset, price is a detail not the prime determinant.

Use analogies. One of the most powerful techniques your salespeople can use to sell your package is analogies. The great communicators fill their rhetoric with analogies, metaphors, and similes. These communications dynamics make it easier for the buyer to understand your message. For example, one company I work with sells cholesterol screening equipment for doctors to perform in-office testing. Because it involves a substantial financial investment, many doctors flinch when they hear the price. The salespeople from this company use analogies to sell the instrument.

It sounds like this: "Doctor Buyer, I realize that four thousand dollars is a significant investment in your practice. We know that with your normal monthly billings after six months the instrument will not only pay for itself, but it will pay for that copier over there. You see, every time you turn on our equipment it's a profit center. Every time you turn on the copier it's a cost center."

What does a copier have to do with a cholesterol screening? Nothing. They remind the doctor that he doesn't mind spending money in an area that costs him. Why would he mind spending money for something that would earn him more money? This is a very strong argument. In fact, they take the analogy a step further to illustrate how profit from the instrument eventually pays for the copier, the cost center.

Look for analogies in the customer's business. If the buyer invests heavily in one area, use it to your advantage. For example, the buyer who remodels his office should invest some advertising money to attract people to see the face-lift. If a restaurant invests heavily in an upscale menu and image enhancement, why wouldn't it invest in a top-quality draft beer for the bar? The list goes on. If I receive a price objection about my fee for meetings, I draw an analogy to how much money the meeting planner spends on food for the attendees' bodies. He should use the same reasoning to feed the group's mind.

These are legitimate comparisons that encourage buyers to reevaluate their present decisions vis-à-vis other buying decisions they've made.

Sell Financially

The difference only. Many times the buyer reacts to the sticker shock of your price. Your salespeople must be able to balance his perspective by presenting the price in its best light. When there is a price difference between you and the competition, refer only to the *difference* in price. If your price is higher than the competition, delete the word "savings" from your vocabulary. The word "difference" implies that your packages are not the same. That's what you want the buyer to hear: "A price difference signals a package difference." Use the price difference as a springboard to discuss other differences.

Miniaturize. Reduce the price difference to the smallest meaningful unit: cost per application, part, person, day, etc. The objective is to point out that the "real" difference is not overwhelming—as the buyer first thought. As you minimize the price, maximize the value. Refer to the total value-added received for the minor difference in price. This casts price in a different light.

Fractionalize. When your product is part of a much bigger package, present the difference in price as a very small part of the total cost. For example, if you sell rice that goes into microwave dinners, weigh the price difference between your rice and the competition's against the total cost of the buyer's producing that meal. Your price may represent a minor part of the total cost. The difference between you and the competition is ludicrously small compared to the total cost. Other "total cost" areas include: the cost of running a department, the total budget for a project, etc. This offers a unique way to view the price difference as minuscule compared to the big picture—especially when you factor in the extra value.

Financial selling is a special skill your salespeople need to differentiate your package from the competition. By learning and applying this skill, your people maximize the difference in value while minimizing the difference in price.

Competitive Selling

To differentiate your package from the competition your salespeople should master competitive selling techniques. This includes spotlighting the differences between you and the competition with presentations built around your unique competitive advantages. This is not "bad-mouthing" the competition. It is presenting your best side, which is coincidentally the competition's weak side.

Begin with a series of questions that alert the buyer to weaknesses in your competitor's package. Typically, these weaknesses are unmet customer needs. This presumes your package satisfies these needs. Once the buyer acknowledges the need for the unique solutions your company offers, support this with your benefits.

To plan your competitive attack, work backward. List your unique advantages (review the VIP list) and design questions that raise these issues. These questions create buyer needs awareness and the motivation to want to change. This is the needs analysis in action.

VALUE-ADDED SUPPORT STRATEGIES

There are a number of support strategies that your sales-people can use to facilitate value-added buying decisions. Some of these are behind-the-scenes ideas while others are front-line strategies. Implementing these strengthens your approach and opens the buyer's mind to value-added solutions.

Create Pull

Basically, there are two ways to market: *push* and *pull*. The difference is in whoever takes the initiative—either the vendor or the customer. If the salesperson contacts the buyer, generates interest in the product, and provides the impetus for the sale, it's push marketing. If the customer initiates contact and actively buys, it's pull marketing. Salesforces are mostly push.

One advantage of pull is that the buyer is more actively involved in the process. She wants to own your product. She is looking for ways to justify the purchase. In many cases, she may be more anxious to buy than you are to sell. Now you have at least two people working to get your product into the customer's account—you and the buyer.

Creating pull in value-added selling is "walking the halls," talking to as many people as possible, and burrowing your way throughout the account like a professional mole. Talk to the influencers, end users, economic buyers, shipping and receiving people—anyone who can put in a good word for you. Create a "customer salesforce" to sell for you when you're not there. View the time you spend with them as sales training. You're training these insiders to help you become an insider. They pull you into the account. Once you've built the rapport, they want you in there and work hard to make it happen.

The value-added salesperson actively looks for ways to build these customer pull relationships. *Teaming* is the strongest way to create pull. Bringing in people from your organization helps. The more people involved in a sale, the less important price becomes. Connect at as many levels as possible. Introduce your technical people to the buyer's technical people; arrange for a meeting between your management and the customer's management; and take your customer service representative on calls to meet her counterpart in the buyer's company. The stronger the alliance between the two companies, the more needs that surface throughout the process that involve more people. And the greater the pull generated because of this strategy, the greater the likelihood that your company will get the business on nonprice issues. Your team has sold value-added.

This valuable "offensive" selling strategy helps you capture new business. As a "defensive" selling strategy, it helps you shut out the competition.

Positioning

Positioning is an advertising term made popular by Ries and Trout in their book *Positioning: The Battle for Your Mind.* Your position is that unique piece of real estate you own inside the customer's head. It's what they think of

when they think of you. To position your company is to
create an attitude toward it in someone else's mind—an
image that comes to one's mind when one thinks about
your company. Everything you do affects this position
either positively or negatively. In value-added selling, it's
imperative that your salespeople use this concept to your
advantage. A simple rule of thumb is: They are either
building it up or breaking it down.

Selling the intangibles. Your salesforce must position your
company as *the* value-added vendor by initiating a campaign to spotlight the wonderful things your company
does. Tell the buyer about your state-of-the-art technology,
new hires in R&D, innovative products coming down the
pike, management commitment to customer satisfaction,
etc. These usually happen in informal but planned ways:
e.g., lunchtime conversations. From the customer's perspective, it's a salesperson talking proudly about her company—a loyal and enthusiastic employee. By itself, this
does not offset price objections, but it is one small "brush
stroke of value-added." Coupled with everything else you
do it's an important part of your strategy.

Use the jargon. Use the "value-added" terminology in the
same sentence with your company's name. Infuse your sales
presentations with "value-added." Include it in correspondence. Tie it to your name. Create a solid association between your company's name and the words "value-added."
Whenever the customer thinks about your company, you
want him to think "value-added." This results from a
concerted positioning effort.

In preparation for working with a Fortune 100 company, I read their annual report. It contained the word
quality twenty-seven times! I had no doubt that they used
quality as their primary competitive weapon. I bench-
marked them as the quality standard for their industry.
Why? Because they said so. They would have to prove
themselves wrong. I assumed they led in quality. They

positioned it that way. Interesting enough, they "owned" the claim of quality. It was theirs to lose!

Value reminders. This is positive bragging. It's looking for a way to brag about all the great things you do for your customer. It's consistently reinforcing the customer's decision to buy from you. Remind the customer that you have gone beyond the call of duty. Be creative and gracious. For most people the purpose of a testimonial letter is to build your case when selling someone. I submit that the real purpose is to remind the buyer that he made a great decision when buying from you. As he writes the letter, he's telling *himself* how good you are. Try something bold. In next year's proposal, include a copy of his own testimonial letter. Brash? Bold? Gutsy? You bet! Who better than himself to remind him that you're great?

If you perform certain services for the buyer, follow up on these to "check" on yourself. While asking "Did we perform for you?" you're reminding the customer that you do deliver. Some salespeople perform quarterly value audits to ensure that the customer is getting maximum usage from the product. Coincidentally, they're reminding the customer of their value. Anything your company does after the sale to reinforce and remind the buyer of your value-added commitment cements the relationship. It goes beyond customer satisfaction: it builds customer loyalty.

The all-time best example of a value reminder comes from one of my customers. His company is a world-renowned quality standard for many industries. In fact, they teach other companies how to increase their quality. They conduct quality seminars as a service to their customers. One of their customers sent everyone in his medium-sized company through this quality program. At the end of the year, the salesperson who manages this account invoiced the customer for $35,000 in training costs. The owner clutched his chest until he saw, at the bottom of the invoice, "No Charge! Part of our Value-Added Service!" How would you like to negotiate next year's contract with a customer and have a $35,000 no-charge invoice in your hand?

Continuously selling the intangibles, using the value-added sales jargon, and reminding the customer of your value positions your company head and shoulders above the competition. This differentiating tactic is integral to your overall value-added business strategy.

Create Barriers

This strategy precludes your being drawn into the price-only scenario. Look for ways to create barriers (differentiating factors) that make it difficult, at best, for the buyer to compare you and the competition. Price shoppers want simple, apples-to-apples comparisons. Your job is to spotlight and celebrate the differences not similarities. Reinforce these differences in three areas: your product, your company, and your salespeople.

Creating barriers should clarify the issues, not confuse the buyer. Creating barriers makes it difficult for the buyer to focus only on generic issues. Some examples include keeping the focus long-term, selling postsale services as the *real* value, demonstrating how you offer lower transitional costs, how your product enables the buyer to increase his competitive posture, and so on.

PROPOSAL TIPS

An important advantage your salespeople can wield is the well-designed proposal. Its appearance and how well your salespeople present it support the perception of greater value. The financial justifications inside prove the quantitative or performance value-added. These tips help you identify the weaknesses in your current system and adapt to give it your best value-added attempt.

Cover Sheet. Dress up your proposal by enclosing it in some type of binder or cover. Remember, value is one part perception. On the first page, the title page, type the customer's name, use his logo if possible, and put your mission statement on the bottom of the page. Let the customer see what your company is all about. Help him experience your commitment to excellence.

Review Needs. Begin your proposal by reviewing past meetings and the needs that surfaced. Discuss these with the customer and get agreement to them before moving on. Invariably, additional needs will surface. This is especially true if other people attend who were not at the original needs-analysis meeting. Once the group agrees to these needs, discuss the consequences of action and inertia. It's reasonable to expect the customer to consider the outcomes of his action or inaction.

Recommendations. This is where every proposal differs in format. Generally, begin with a statement about objectives. Include long- and short-term buying objectives. Long-term objectives refocus the price shopper. Once the buyer focuses long-term, state your expectations for results.

Fees and Terms. On this page, include your terms and conditions. Include as many *no-charge* items as possible. The more no-charge items the greater the perceived value. Include special purchasing terms that save the customer money: for example, prepaid terms or 2 percent, ten days.

Support. In this section, include anything that strengthens your proposal: testimonial letters, data and statistics tables, value analysis justification, warranties or guarantees, and most importantly—a personal letter of commitment from you (the salesperson) to the buyer. This letter details your commitment (as the salesperson) to the buyer for her business. It's your way of saying, "If you go with me, I commit to do this for you." This is a powerful demonstration of sales professionalism. And *no one* is doing it currently!

CHAPTER SUMMARY

In this chapter, I focused on how you can train your salespeople to approach the customer proactively. The message was simple—build in enough value on the front end to preempt price on the back end. The more proactive your salespeople become the less direct supervision they'll need in the future. When they acquire the habit of initiative, they're asking themselves how they can enhance your package for the customer. Value-added is a philosophy of maximum performance not minimum standards. With that mindset firmly entrenched at the field level, you'll unleash the full power of professional selling at its best.

3
The Critical Buying Path

The fundamental problem salespeople experience is reflected in what a salesperson said to me one day in a seminar. "Tom, we already know that we should sell value-added. It's our customers who need a seminar—on buying value-added!" The group laughed at this simplistic explanation of his predicament with price shoppers. And yet, he was on to something. Salespeople do need a way to educate buyers to make better buying decisions. This is a primary function of value-added selling—to assist, educate, and sophisticate buyers to make prudent long-term decisions.

Buyer behavior reflects inner emotions. It's the manifestation of right-brain emotional and left-brain rational issues. Buyers grapple with what appears to be sometimes conflicting internal motives. Multiply this by the number of people involved in the decision process and you get an idea of the stress buyers experience. This inner dialogue of rational/emotional voices coupled with external forces ultimately influences the customer's definition of value. Value is always customer-driven. You don't know what it is until the customer defines it. The degree to which you perceive and conceive as buyers affects your understanding of value-added. Feeling what the customer feels and seeing what he sees impassions you to deliver your message with conviction and enthusiasm.

A clear understanding of needs, wants, and desires motivates a different buying decision than fuzzy thinking. Buyers translate this information into some type of decision-making process. Simple needs require a simple solution. Complex needs require more sophisticated decisions. Regardless of the need, buyers go through a process to decide—simple or complex.

Buyer needs go beyond acquisition. They have ownership and usage needs. Until now, most salespeople considered these separate from the decision-making process. I submit that when you consolidate these needs and educate the buyer that this is an ownership process—not disconnected needs—you have a tremendous potential to sell value-added. This process begins with the existence of a need. It extends through ordering, reordering, usage, and service. These needs are synergistic—connected and whole.

WHAT IS THE CRITICAL BUYING PATH?

The *Critical Buying Path* is a buying and usage process. It is all the steps your customers go through from the moment that a need exists up to and including using your product, getting service, and disposal. It's a model that naturally flows from need to satisfaction. It's a dynamic, interactive, and overlapping sequence of events. It changes from customer to customer and industry to industry.

Sophisticated purchases have a longer and more detailed Path. Less sophisticated buying decisions require a simpler Path. For example, selling mainframe computers involves a protracted sales cycle and many people from both sides. This Path may have twenty or thirty steps in it. On the other hand, buying an automobile is far simpler and involves fewer steps. Both scenarios have one thing in common: their buyers go through a decision and usage process that extends from the moment the need *exists* (not surfaces) up to and including disposal of what they are about to buy.

Please reread the last sentence in the previous paragraph. *We have redefined the sale.* The sale begins the moment a need exists—not necessarily in the customer's mind but in reality—and isn't over until whatever you sell has worn out or is being replaced for some other reason. Salespeople who understand and accept their redefined role within the Critical Buying Path model and work to convince buyers that their needs extend beyond acquisition have the unique opportunity to sell value-added. This is twenty-first-century selling.

As you train your salespeople on the Path, they experience value-added as "value received," i.e., from the customer's perspective. Experiencing value-added this way validates your solution. It builds salesforce empathy and confidence to see value from the customer's vantage point. Cost justification for your solution is a natural part of this model. Your salesforce appreciates the financial impact of your solution when they juxtapose it to customer needs.

The Path is also a brainstorming model. As your people view the buying and owning process in microcosm, they discover ways for your company to add even more value for the customer. As they educate the buyer on this model's jargon, they're creating a language that's foreign to the competition.

Need Exists

This is the static phase of the sale. The buyer is doing nothing to satisfy the need. Customer apathy or lack of insight may be your competition at this point. To sell value-added you must presume that you offer a solution for some unmet need within the buyer's environment. The buyer may not be consciously aware of this need. But, on an unconscious level, he feels some dissatisfaction and satisfaction with the status quo. He may be in a comfort zone because he's unaware of how the unmet need affects him. Buyers, like most people, resist change. They cling desperately to the old, the familiar, and the comfortable. Until the dissatisfaction level is higher than the satisfaction level, they are motivated to stay with the status quo. The dissatisfaction level is a catalyst to change and you are the change agent. Help your buyer feel this dissatisfaction. Creating an objective needs awareness for the buyer is the first step in convincing him to change.

Planning Stage

This is the presale activities stage of the Path. The customer's greatest need at this stage is for clarification of needs and potential solutions. He's in an information-seeking mode. The computer metaphor is a great way to conceive of what's happening here. Customers input facts from a variety of sources—internal staff, suppliers, third-party references, etc. They process this information in the decision-making phase and output a desired solution. The value-added salesperson enters this stage as early as possible— ideally during input. The more input the salesperson has in the early stages the greater her impact on the outcome of the sale.

The planning stage is formally divided into three substeps: *study, source,* and *select.* Even though these steps appear linear, they overlap. Studying and sourcing are roughly equivalent to the computer input and processing stages while selecting is similar to outputting.

Study

Ultimately, the buyer must answer this question: "What's needed and why?" The answer lies outside and inside the buyer's organization. First, to determine his needs accurately, a buyer performs a *situation analysis*. He looks outward assessing industry conditions, competitive pressures, his buyers' preferences, and his company's vulnerability in the marketplace. Studying these influences gives the buyer greater insight into the driving forces behind his needs. They may explain why and when he must act.

The second, albeit connected, part of his analysis is internal. This internal needs analysis examines the symptoms and causes of these problems. For this information, the buyer gathers facts from a variety of sources. He conducts internal meetings to discuss the problems and brainstorm for solutions. He builds expectations by listing the things he would *like* to have and the things he *must* have.

Once the buyer performs the situation analysis, the next step is to create a *statement of needs*. Using the information discovered in the situation analysis, the buyer writes specifications for ideal solutions, establishes parameters, determines areas of flexibility, sets long- and short-term goals, allocates budgets, and outlines buying objectives.

You've just experienced the "ideal" buyer. Unfortunately, it doesn't always work out this way. Many buyers go into the decision process with considerably less information about their needs than for potential solutions. Their greatest need at this point is for clarification of their personal situation. Any way your company facilitates this insight is a bonus for your competitive advantage. The results of the study phase are buying parameters. The earlier you enter this process the more likely you are to help write these purchasing guidelines. The questions you ask raise the buyer's awareness of enhanced needs. The answers you provide later convince him that you offer value-added solutions.

Source

As introspective as the study phase is, the source phase is "extraspective." The focus is off his problems and onto potential solutions. He's searching for options by asking and answering the question, "What's available and from whom?" Even with internal solutions available, the buyer often solicits outside help.

Sourcing is noise reduction. With many available options, the buyer must prescreen them for viability. It's the first cut. This preliminary search-and-screen mission focuses on meeting minimum standards of performance. If the potential solution meets minimum viability standards, the buyer keeps it for additional scrutiny. Crucial to the success of this approach is the involvement of influencers, end users, and decision makers in the process. They pretest the solutions against prescribed buying criteria.

Select

Selecting the most viable alternative answers the question, "Which is the best option and why?" This is the second cut. It begins with a request for proposals (RFP) and continues through the formal decision-making process. This varies from company to company but there are similarities in the method. Committees meet to weigh the various alternatives, perform cost analyses and justifications, and make recommendations. It usually involves a decision/revision process.

The buyer may change specifications, rework budgets, and test these against the original standards. This decision/revision process naturally culminates in awarding the business to the most viable alternative.

Acquisition Stage

The acquisition stage is the transitional phase of ownership. It's those activities that prepare buyers to own and use a product. During acquisition, the buyer wants smooth transitions—whatever it takes to prepare for receiving and using the goods. Facility, expediency, and simplicity are critical to this phase. It begins with the award and includes preinstallation and installation.

Award

This overlaps the planning stage. It's generating the orders, processing requests, signing the contracts, physically writing the order, verbal POs, electronic and voice-mail ordering, order confirmation, back-order reports, shipping advice, and coordinating delivery schedules.

Preinstallation

Once the order is entered and confirmed, the buyer prepares for delivery. Resource preparation includes people and facilities. Preparing employees addresses their skills deficiencies and emotional needs. There are identifiable and measurable skills needed when transitioning from one system or product to another. Training classes bridge this knowledge gap.

Additionally, people have emotional ties to the old way. Prudent buyers recognize and accept this. By understanding that some employees cling to the past unless they've had an opportunity to adjust to the new motivates some buyers to use the transitioning phase to prepare employees for change. They involve employees in the process and build ownership while lowering resistance to change.

While attending to employees, buyers also prepare the facility for change. This includes simple things like making room for additional inventory and complex things like modifying an entire production facility for the new product—and everything in-between.

Installation

The facility and employees are ready for the change—the "plug-in" date. Installation is where the buyer accepts delivery of goods, transfers, unpacks, verifies code numbers, checks for breakage, pretests, arranges for returns and credits, assembles the product, and familiarizes employees with the new system. This may involve additional training. The buyer is now prepared to use the product for its intended purpose.

Usage Stage

"People don't buy quarter-inch drills—they buy quarter-inch holes." Buyers purchase something for what it does for them: the end result, the benefit. This is the usage stage. During usage, the buyer wants economy and enhancement. Economy refers to effort, operational costs, and time. Enhancement refers to productivity and expansion. There are two main activities in the usage stage: *transformation* and *growth*.

Transformation

This is the "now" phase, the up-and-running phase. The buyer wants to use the product for its intended purpose. This means transforming it by producing something else, using it "as is," or reselling it to someone. It creates another product or profit for the buyer. One goal of transformation is maximum economy of time, money, and effort. The buyer wants to produce results with minimum investment on his part.

Another goal of transformation is maximum productivity. The buyer wants a significant return on his investment: the most from something—whether it's higher quality, tighter specifications, or quicker results. Performance is the objective.

Other transformation issues include service concerns: getting replacement parts, repairs, reordering materials, technical assistance, sales and marketing help for distributors, end-user training and support, reinstallation at the field level, etc. The magnitude of the support needed depends on the sophistication of the sale. A telecommunications buyer needs more help at this point than a new-car purchaser.

Growth

This is the "future" phase, the down-the-road phase. The value-added buyer thinks, plans, and acts long-term. He is proactive. A major concern for him is future growth. He wants gain, increase, and expansion and pursues it aggressively.

Model Recap

The Critical Buying Path is strictly customer driven. It's how the buyer experiences value-added vis-à-vis buying decisions. It begins with the existence of a need and proceeds on to how the buyer plans to handle the need, acquisition issues, and receiving maximum performance from the solution. If you view the Path as a model for adding value, you're in a unique position to sell your value-added package to the customer.

HOW SALESPEOPLE FIT INTO THE CRITICAL BUYING PATH

One of the great advantages of this model is recognizing how the salesperson's role changes over the Path. By training your salespeople to switch hats throughout this process, you're preparing them to add maximum value while differentiating themselves from the competition. In the next sections, I explain how the salesperson's role changes and which skills he needs at each step along the way.

Needs Exist

Because this is the static phase of the sale and the buyer may be doing nothing to satisfy the need, the salesperson prepares himself to convince the buyer that a need exists. Much of the activity is behind the scenes. In Chapter 2, I introduced two important skills your salespeople need for the planning stage:

1. Building their knowledge base
2. Leveraging their sales time with Jumbo CDs

Your salespeople study to build their knowledge base while increasing their sales equity to the buyer. The strategic value analysis from Chapter 2 is a great place to start. The mental capital they accumulate during this process is useful along the Path. This is a personal investment in value-added that your salesforce contributes to the sale.

While building her knowledge, the salesperson leverages her sales time by focusing on viable prospects—Jumbo CD buyers. Once she targets these accounts, she begins precall positioning by sending company literature, constructing powerful sales letters that spotlight value-added benefits, and sending articles about her company. This sales/marketing effort paves the way for additional differentiation later in the Path. It creates the expectation that this salesperson is a cut above everyone else—barriers for the competition. An apples-to-apples comparison is difficult at best.

Planning Stage

Because the buyer's greatest need at this point is clarification and information, the salesperson is an information conduit: gathering and giving information. This is the *sales mode*. The salesperson has two very specific objectives for this stage of the Path. First, he educates the buyer how to make informed buying decisions. He's selling the buyer on the concept of value-added purchasing. The premise is simple. If the salesperson convinces the buyer to make buying decisions based on enhanced needs, the buyer recognizes and welcomes value-added solutions. The salesperson relies heavily on many of the skills outlined in Chapter 2:

- Performing the customer audit (the needs analysis)
- Creating pull

Since the objective is to raise the buyer's awareness that he has enhanced needs requiring value-added solutions, the needs analysis plays a major role in the planning stage. Teach your salespeople to probe proactively with the twenty-five questions listed in Chapter 2, look for buyer pressure points, and burrow deep into the account. Creating this objective needs awareness is fundamental to convincing the buyer to make long-range value-added decisions.

Your salespeople build support for their case by involving many people in the decision process. As end users contribute their perspectives, the buying criteria changes to reflect the *total* organization's needs. Bringing in vendor experts (e.g., your technical people) to help sell the concept is an important part of the pull process. As buyer employees ally themselves with vendor counterparts, strong teams form toward a common mission: the most viable solution for the customer. An interesting dynamic of this process is the burgeoning trust. As trust grows, price becomes less important.

While clarifying the buyer's perception of needs and creating pull, the salesperson's second objective is to present unique ideas to convince the buyer of the seller's value-added status. The salesperson differentiates his company with three important skills covered in Chapter 2:

1. Positioning
2. Presenting
3. Competitive selling

Positioning is distancing your company from the pack by focusing on unique advantages. Company literature, targeted sales presentations, and other marketing support materials are great places to start.

Teach your salespeople to present with punch. Use the tips listed in the previous chapter to enhance their presentations. Include financial selling tips that cost-justify the buying decision. Offer proof that your company is the best long-term decision. Dress up your proposals to boost perceived value. All steaks must sizzle!

Be bold in this stage. Encourage your salespeople to spotlight the differences in your package. Use tough competitive probes that raise doubts about other alternatives. Create barriers that discourage apples-to-apples comparisons. Your salespeople can sell competitively without bad-mouthing the competition. They need your guidance and permission.

Acquisition Stage

During this stage, the salesperson is in the *operations mode*. Since the buyer's most compelling need is smooth transitions, the focus shifts from fact-finding, showing, and talking to ensuring that ordering, shipping/receiving, and installation go smoothly. The salesperson wears two different hats at this point. First, he is a change agent helping the customer prepare employees and systems for the new solution. Second, the salesperson plays the coordinator role—handling logistics issues.

The skills most needed at this time are relating skills to help employees cope with change. This includes listening to concerns and doubts, human-relations skills to help train those affected by the change, and internal selling skills within your organization. This last skills set is especially important when attempting to expedite results.

Organizational skills like scheduling, follow-up, and troubleshooting play a key role at this point along the Path. Customers expect salespeople to have at their fingertips order status information. This reassures the buyer that she made the right decision to go with this vendor. This is commonsense "Golden Rule" service that most people want and deserve from suppliers.

Usage Stage

Until now, we've focused on offensive selling skills: gaining new business. In the usage stage, the customer wants maximum economy, performance, and growth. The salesperson's objective changes. He is now in the *service mode*. Assuring that customers receive that which they expect is paramount to success. From this perspective, the salesperson is a service specialist. He assures customer satisfaction. The best strategy for tomorrow is to ensure that today's customer is getting maximum return on his investment.

Increasing the customer's business is one of the best offensive and defensive selling strategies for salespeople. It's easier to sell satisfied customers. The Chapter 2 skills to emphasize are:

- Value reminding
- Opportunity probing

Every salesperson must review with the customer how much value the supplier delivers. This ensures that customer expectations are being met and that the supplier gets his just credits. It's a double win. Reviewing and reminding the customer works best when it becomes a routine part of the sales cycle.

While reviewing past successes, salespeople look to the future by probing into growth areas with the customer. Focusing on expansion and growth, the salesperson ensures his role in the process. Pursuing these opportunities with new products and services is cost-effective for buyers and sellers. It conserves the buyer's resources and keeps the selling costs down. Cross-selling and consolidating purchases is one of the most economical and value-added ways for two people to do business.

Figure 3 summarizes what occurs along the Critical Buying Path. The buyer has certain objectives and the seller has concomitant objectives. In both cases, activities

FIGURE 3
CRITICAL BUYING PATH™

CUSTOMER NEEDS		SALESPERSON'S ROLE
During this phase of the Path, the customer's greatest need is clarification: problems, needs, solutions, and vendors. This involves a massive information drive.	PLANNING	*Sales Mode* During this phase of the Path, the salesperson is an information conduit, gathering and giving information.
During acquisition, the buyer wants smooth transitions: facility, expediency, and simplicity are critical.	ACQUISITION	*Operations Mode* During this phase, the salesperson plays the coordinator role. The focus shifts from fact-finding, showing, and talking to ensuring that ordering, logistics, and installation are handled smoothly.
During usage, the customer wants economy and enhancement. Economy refers to effort, operational costs, and time. Enhancement refers to growth and expansion.	USAGE	*Service Mode* At this phase, the salesperson is a usage and growth specialist. He helps the customer achieve maximum economy in utilization and paves the way for future growth.

support these objectives. Figure 4 is a blank Path for you to complete with your salesforce. Discuss the model and have your group customize it for your industry and customers. If you experience some difficulty performing this exercise, think of a specific account that purchases with a value-added focus. Outline the steps from the moment a need surfaces through planning, acquisition, and usage. You'll notice how difficult it is to get consensus from your group on this. This signals how many different Critical Buying Paths there are.

If possible, estimate how much each step costs the customer. You're attempting to attach a dollar figure to your customer's purchasing activities. By doing this, you're "tangibilizing" or cost-justifying your value-added along the Path. I cover this more fully in the next section.

FIGURE 4
CRITICAL BUYING PATH™

This is the "ideal" Critical Buying Path for your buyers. On the left side, outline the buyer's steps. On the right side, list your company's value-added:

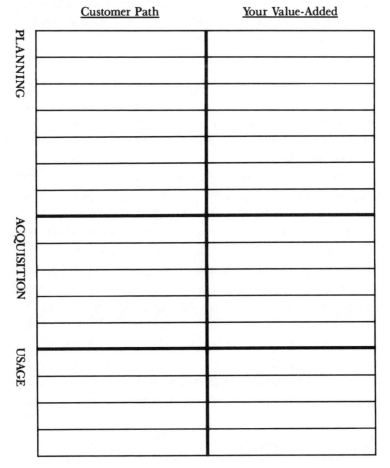

HOW TO ADD VALUE

Many salespeople cheat themselves by not taking full advantage of or getting credit for the value-added they offer. Other salespeople miss significant opportunities to add even more value-added because they are not trained to think in these terms. First, this section helps you train your salespeople to recognize how your value-added plays along the Path. By juxtaposing your value-added to the customer's needs along the Path, your salespeople get a realistic perspective on what your company really brings to the table. Second, this section provides you with some great brainstorming ideas for determining where you can add even more value to the sale.

Current Value-Added

Now that your salespeople have a customized Path, you're ready to insert your value-added along it. This is the acid test. You must determine if your value-added is as important from the customer's perspective as you believe it is. Refer to your VIP list. From this list, select those value-added extras that fit into the planning stage.

Rank them in chronological order (in Figure 4) from the customer's perspective. Begin with those value-added extras that are relevant to the study phase. Which of your VIP items answer the customer's question, "What's needed and why?" List these along the right side of the Path. If your company offers the customer a service for identifying market conditions, trends, etc., this is value-added and relevant to the study phase. If your company offers an in-depth needs analysis for the customer as part of your package, this is also relevant to the study phase. List it here.

Continue this process throughout the rest of the planning stage—sourcing and selection. Which part of your bundled package addresses the buyer's sourcing question,

"What's available and from whom?" Does your company offer a competitive profile that explains the differences between you and your competition? Does your literature make it easy for the buyer to focus on your value-added? He needs competitive intelligence. Your challenge is to satisfy that need and simultaneously position your company as the value-added supplier.

What value-added in your package answers the selection question, "Which is the best option and why?" At this point, the buyer is evaluating your package vis-à-vis the competition. Deciding on a final option at this point may involve changing specs to fit the alternatives, allocating more funding, testing the revised specs, etc. List your value-added here that supports these issues.

After completing the right-hand side of the page for the planning stage, repeat the drill for the acquisition and usage stages. Stay focused on the buyer's goals in both stages. In the acquisition stage, list your value-added that facilitates smooth transitions. The customer wants order placement to go smoothly. How does your value support this? During preinstallation, the buyer prepares his people and systems. Include anything you offer to help in this area. Because he wants to install quickly and smoothly, determine which of your value-added extras contribute to this goal. List them on the right side.

During usage, the buyer wants maximum economy, productivity, and growth. List your value-added that assists him in achieving these goals. Include follow-up visits to ensure customer satisfaction, business reviews that recap successes and guide future development, and suggestions for better utilization of your product. How have you helped him better use what you sold?

You should begin to see an emerging pattern at this point. Most companies front-end load their value-added—before and during installation. You've just created a visual chronology of your company's value-added. Ask yourself these four questions to get an accurate picture of where you are:

1. Where are we strong?
2. Where are we weak?
3. For each value-added extra we deliver, can we ascertain the real savings to the customer along the Path? (Are we selling this savings as a profit enhancement for the customer?)
4. Where do our greatest opportunities for VIP enhancement exist?

This last question is critical. It points to the future . . . additional value you could potentially bring to the table.

Adding More Value

This next brainstorming exercise helps you and your staff create the future by adding value. Initially generate a *quantity* of ideas. Eventually, you test these for viability. The entire exercise centers around these three umbrella questions:

1. What can we do to make it easier for the buyer to understand his needs and *plan* for his purchase?
2. How can we make it easier for the buyer to *acquire* and prepare to use our package?
3. How can we help the customer better *use* what we sell him to gain maximum return on his investment?

These three major questions focus on the three stages of the Path. To get more specific ideas, parallel your questions to each step in your customer's typical Path. This focuses you on industry-specific purchasing needs. Then, ask yourself the brainstorming question, "What can we do to make the customer's life easier at this point?" The answer to this question is the seed of a new value-added idea.

It doesn't even need to be a good idea at this point, just an idea. By the time you cook it, process it, scrutinize it, test it, retest it, package it, sell it, and get credit for it, the finished product idea may barely resemble the initial brainstorming thought.

Critical Impact Questions

The following list of questions "prime the pump." They are neither exhaustive nor should they supplant your industry-specific Path questions. I call these *critical impact questions* because they point to general areas where you can have an impact on the customer's business. Consider these a great jumping-off point for your value-added brainstorming exercise.

- How can we help the customer better understand his problem?
- Is there a way we can help the customer collect all relevant information regarding his problem situation?
- In what ways can I help the customer design specifications for his problem situation?
- How can we help get information regarding our solution to all relevant parties within the customer's business (that is, play the coordinator role)?
- What can our company do to make ordering easier for the customer?
- How can we package or ship our goods to make the customer's life easier?
- Is there something we can do to help the customer receive, warehouse, or ship internally the goods that we sell them?
- How can we expedite return goods, issue credit, and reship with the least negative impact on the customer?

- What can we do to help the customer use, convert, or supply our product more efficiently and productively (i.e., gain quick maximum usage of our product)?
- If service concerns arise after the sale, what can we do to expedite quick resolution of these concerns?

If your customer sells to someone else, also ask these questions:

- How can we help our customers get their message out more effectively?
- Can we do something that expedites and simplifies the "end user's" ordering from our customers?
- How can our company help our customer in distribution of his (our) product to his customers?
- Is there a way we can help the end user get quick and courteous service after the sale?
- Do we need to concern ourselves with end users needing repair or replacement parts?

Evaluation Matrix

You've generated a list of possible value-added extras. Now you're ready to test these ideas for viability. These ideas offer your company hope for the future—the seeds of differentiation. To see how they'll grow and if you'll be able to harvest them, you must "reality-test" these ideas against predetermined viability criteria. Use these questions as guidelines for qualifying your "seeds of differentiation."

- What is the financial *cost* of implementing these ideas?
- How long (*time*) will it take to implement these ideas?
- How *easy* are they to implement?
- Will the customer value (*receptiveness*) these ideas?
- Can we do it?

FIGURE 5
EVALUATION MATRIX

VALUE-ADDED IDEAS	COST	IMPLEMENTATION EASE	CUSTOMER PERCEPTION OF VALUE	TIME	OTHER	TOTALS	RANK
1.							
2.							
3.							
4.							
5.							
6.							
7.							
8.							

1 = Desirable   2 = OK   3 = Undesirable

Include company and industry-specific questions that test the viability of these ideas. The *evaluation matrix* (see Figure 5) expedites your assessment. It is an opportunity for your salespeople to get their day in court. It helps you explain why you can or cannot implement suggested value-added extras. Overall, it facilitates group understanding for making better business decisions while pursuing opportunities to further differentiate your company.

USAGE TIPS

The Path is one of the most creative insights into value-added selling you can share with your salespeople. Helping them understand how to apply it gives them a competitive advantage that's hard to match. These usage tips offer concrete application examples.

Since one of the salesperson's early objectives is to sell the buyer on making a more informed value-oriented buying decision, construct a list of the twelve most important questions that a value-added buyer in your industry should ask himself before making a final decision. These questions naturally parallel the Path steps we discussed earlier. The more industry-specific you can make this the greater the likelihood that the buyer will use it.

Remember, these are questions that a buyer would ask himself from *his* perspective. These questions call attention to the fact that the buyer has many needs (enhanced needs) that transcend the generic. These also call attention to areas where your company offers unique value-added extras. You could publish a booklet entitled "The Twelve Most Important Things Buyers Should Ask Themselves when Purchasing."

Another idea is to compile a list of these questions and give it to the buyer early in the sales cycle (i.e., the Path). The salesperson tells the buyer that this is a list of questions you compiled from buyers in your industry. Explain how other customers have praised this list for helping them view the whole picture.

A third and more sophisticated application is the "Value-Added Purchasing Manual." Create a manual for customers that parallels their buying procedure and make each section of the binder a separate step along the Path. Naturally, you're walking the buyer through the buying process and helping him understand the totality of his needs. The thought-provoking questions and inspiring benefits you offer in each section lead him to the obvious conclusion that your option is the best alternative for his company.

Once you construct this manual, train your salespeople on how to persuade buyers to use it. Tell the buyer this is something your company developed based on years of working with other customers to help them maximize the value they receive from a purchase. The net gain for the buyer is that he receives additional insight into the decision process. It helps him make a better buying decision.

Present this as a benefit to him. Introduce this concept early in the decision process as part of the value-added your company offers . . . just part of the service!

CHAPTER SUMMARY

In this chapter, we focused on value-added from the customer's perspective. I call this value received. The Critical Buying Path is a model to help you better understand how customers perceive and receive value. This gives you a tool to train your salespeople how to get inside the customer's skin.

The Path is an excellent tool for analyzing your company's value and impact on the customer. It's possible to use this model to determine the financial impact your package represents. The Path can also be used as a planning tool to help you identify where your company can add even more value.

As you explain this concept to your salesforce, demonstrate how their roles change along the Path. Illustrate how they provide information in the sales mode, smooth things out in the operations mode, and assure satisfaction in the service mode. It is a useful tool for helping your people redefine the sale and clarify their roles in the process. More important, it helps them view your solution from the buyer's perspective—value received.

4
Handling Price Resistance

How do you persist without being a pest? This is the most fundamental question salespeople must ask and answer to respond effectively to price objections. Three out of every four salespeople quit with the first buyer "No." Another 5 percent quit after the second negative response. A scant 20 percent persist for the third no. The objective is not to get three no's—it's to persist in a fashion that answers the buyer's objection so thoroughly that he wants to buy (without jamming the product down his throat).

Persistence is the underlying dynamic for successfully responding to objections, yet few salespeople understand its power. A purchasing agent was in my value-added selling seminar one day when the topic of persistence surfaced. He raised his hand and said, "Tom, I don't like persistent salespeople!"

I responded with, "I don't like pushy salespeople."

He said, "That's the same thing."

"No, it's not," I countered. He had this puzzled look on his face, so I continued. "If I asked for your business but caved in at the first sight of resistance, what would you think."

"That you didn't care very much," he conceded.

I argued my point further. "If I don't have the guts to hang in there and fight for your business when it represents an order for me, how in the world will I ever go to bat for you if there's a problem after the sale?"

He thought about it and said, "I never looked at it that way before."

Hallelujah, we have a convert, I thought.

He clearly understood the importance of persistence. He didn't want to deal with low-assertive salespeople who would fail to persist for him if he needed help getting something from the salesperson's company. He wanted people who would pursue his objectives just as aggressively as they pursue their own.

Another buyer added a slightly different spin to this persistent/pushy issue. He characterized "the pushy salesperson as the individual who relentlessly pursues the sale after it's dead with a host of canned rebuttals. This salesperson does not actively listen to the buyer's question or objection—he merely works to jam it down the customer's throat."

The persistent salesperson listens carefully to the buyer's reason for hesitating, empathizes with the customer, and provides a well-thought, relevant answer that reflects her understanding of the buyer's concern. She's fighting for her business in a way that tells the buyer she's concerned about a double win.

Teach your salespeople to be persistent without being a pest. Responding to objections is one of the most difficult things for salespeople to do. Answering price objections is especially challenging. It's the most common objection salespeople bring to seminars yet the one they are least prepared to handle. That was the motivation for writing my first book, *Value-Added Selling Techniques*. I wanted to help salespeople effectively deal with this objection.

This chapter is about hope. It's about open and persuasive communication with the customer. I present a simple and powerful three-step communication model for responding to objections, specific answer strategies for price situations, and value-added negotiating tips for salespeople.

TIPS FOR OBJECTIONS

Anticipate objections positively. Expect them but don't create them. Be prepared for them by having an objections file. This is a list of responses to the most frequently heard objections your salespeople encounter. List the top ten with two or three responses per objection. When you give this to your staff, it's like Christmas because of their excitement about receiving this list. This simple preparation exercise builds confidence through competence.

Teach your staff to divorce their egos from the sale. When the buyer says "No," it isn't a personal attack on the salesperson. Defensive salespeople do not think clearly. They are unable to give the buyer and themselves the benefit of an appropriate response. Listening helps.

Actively listening to the buyer's objection gives your people time to think while diagnosing the real objection. It's difficult to appear defensive while using your ears instead of your mouth. Train your people to listen for what's being said and not said. Alert them to the buyer's nonverbal clues. Is something obvious because it is not mentioned? Teach your folks to use their ears twice as much as their mouths.

Explain to your salesforce that persistence can be a positive energy force. Give them permission to persist. Tell them it's okay to dig when they hear an objection. If they are hesitant to persist because they don't want to be perceived as pushy, convince them that buyers want to deal with assertive and confident salespeople. The following response is especially powerful for those scenarios when the salesperson feels he is perceived as pushy. "Ms. Buyer, I understand that I am aggressive in pursuing this. That's because I'm interested in your business. And there's a flip-side benefit to this. If there's ever a problem after the sale, I'll be just as aggressive to get it solved." You've turned a potentially negative quality into an advantage to the customer.

There are times when your salespeople must help the buyer save face. Because the buyer may have misunderstood something, he may object for all the wrong, albeit legitimate, reasons in his mind. Train your salespeople to minimize the impact of correcting the buyer by assuming partial responsibility for the misunderstanding. It's much easier for people to change their minds when they realize that someone else is responsible for the error. A simple "Perhaps I was unclear in my explanation" goes a long way toward helping the buyer save face and the salesperson save the order. Imagine the contrast between this statement and the following: "Wait a minute, you didn't understand what I said. . . ." The latter alienates while the first engages.

THREE-STEP MODEL

A major advantage of this model is the confidence it builds to handle many different situations. A tactics-driven response to objections means that you must have in your arsenal several canned responses to a multitude of objections. The *model approach* is built on a different set of assumptions. Using the model approach encourages a more conceptual understanding of the objection. This encourages your salesforce to think through the resistance and offer an appropriate response. Buyers perceive the difference between canned rebuttals and insightful answers.

Responding to any objection requires your salespeople to really hear and feel the objection from the customer's perspective, acknowledge this understanding, and respond appropriately: clarify, buffer, and answer.

Clarify

Clarifying an objection is building understanding and appreciation for the customer's point of view. One way to clarify an objection is to dig deeper to understand better what the other person is saying. Keep him talking. Allow him to vent fully. Encourage the buyer to elaborate. Digging deeper is asking the question, "Why?" There must be a hundred ways to ask the buyer why he is hesitating.

When you probe an objection, you demonstrate that you care enough to want to hear the buyer. You avoid the canned response, and the other person notices this. Active buyer involvement helps vent some of the concern and frustration he may be feeling. It also gives you time to consider your response and prevents you from using the firehose approach to objections—that is, blasting him with a spray of benefits.

Here are some examples of clarifiers:

- "I'm curious why you feel that way."
- "Could you be more specific, please?"
- "Do you need more time or more information?"
- "How would that affect your decision?"

In each case, the clarifier is an open-ended question. You want the other person to expound. Expose hidden objections. Help the buyer volunteer additional information that makes your response more meaningful.

A price objection could mean several things. Is the buyer objecting to the price or the package? Maybe the price is not high—rather, the package is not good enough. He doesn't agree that your package is worth the price. A price objection could mean that the buyer may not have the funding. Another possibility is that he is attempting to make an apples-to-apples comparison for unlike products. Is your competition that much cheaper? Or is the buyer exaggerating? Some buyers even throw up smoke screens to stall for another reason—how about bad credit?

It's reasonable to assume that buyers are conditioned to ask for a better price. You could be dealing with a conditioned buying response that has very little to do with your actual price. Think about it. There are so many possibilities for price resistance that your salespeople must dig deeper when they encounter obstacles. You cannot answer that which you do not understand.

Clarifying an objection also means restating the objection in your own words, reframing it as a question you can answer. This demonstrates that you hear the buyer and understand his hesitation. For example:

- "So you're asking why you should pay more for our solution versus the competition's product?"
- "You're concerned that our product will meet all of your needs?"
- "Is it really a question of why you should go with our product line when the other one you're using is OK?"

In each of these examples, you demonstrate that you hear the objection and are prepared to answer the question.

Buffer

Let the buyer know that you're on his side . . . that this does not need to be adversarial. Everyone is entitled to his or her own doubts. Even buyers of your products. A *buffer* shows empathy and neutralizes the friction. With a buffer, you partially agree with the buyer. Let him know that you understand *his right* to hesitate. You're not legitimizing the objection—only his right to have an opinion. The following examples demonstrate partial agreement with the buyer:

- "I hear you."
- "Money is one consideration." (Not the *only* consideration)
- "Making a timely decision for this project is very important."
- "Many of our existing customers asked the same question initially."

Notice that I never tell the buyer that his objection is correct. Rather, I let him know I appreciate his point of view. His accepting this buffer carries with it the implied understanding that he'll listen to my point of view. Also, notice that each one of these buffers is like an incomplete sentence. Something follows. That's the "answer" strategy that I cover in the next section.

Resist the tendency to use the "Yes/but" technique. "Yes, Ms. Buyer, I hear you, *but* . . ." *But* negates everything that precedes it. It's a take-away technique. This escalates the antagonism your buyer already feels. Train your salespeople to replace *but* with *and. And* acknowledges the buyer's opinion while paving the way for the salesperson to express his viewpoint. For example, "Yes, Ms. Prospect, I understand your concern for economy, *and* another thing to consider is . . ." Partial agreement and redirecting the buyer to relevant cost-justification examples salvages this sale.

These examples offer some perspective on how the clarifier and the buffer work together:

(Customer objection) "I want to think about it."
(Clarifier) "What specifically do you need to think about?"

(Customer response) "I must be sure that this is the best decision."

(Buffer) "I understand that you want the best solution for your needs."

This flows very naturally because it's a communication skill. It works because it facilitates the conversation and prevents the salesperson from becoming defensive and argumentative.

Answer

Responding to objections is simple . . . theoretically. Making it work effectively is another story. You either *get* more information to help you better understand the customer's needs, *give* more information to correct or convince, or you walk away from the business. Generally, this is what happens. Specifically, price objections require some additional ideas.

Value Subtraction. This is the opposite of value-added. Reduce your package to fit the buyer's budget. Another option is to substitute a less expensive alternative. The shock value of your changing the package redirects the buyer to his primary objective: to get a value-added solution addressing all of his needs versus a limited response that only meets his price objective. For example:

> Mr. Prospect, if your primary concern is budget, maybe there is a way we can get some of the value from our package to meet the price you're willing to pay.

Then, systematically reduce and change your package until it fits the price he is willing to pay. Some buyers begin to rebuild the solution to fit all their needs. Other shoppers tell you that the value-reduced package is exactly what they want. Give it to them. Perhaps you initially overestimated their needs. Others try to negotiate for the enhanced package at the reduced price.

Cast Doubt. When you're selling to existing customers who have experienced your service, capitalize on it and remind them of the security it offers them. Your company is the known entity. The competition is the unknown. Seventy percent of the people with whom you deal are low-risk individuals. Point out the unknown:

> Ms. Customer, we know what it will cost if you pay a little more to go with our guaranteed service. That's the "known" entity. The only "unknown" in this scenario is what you miss by not going with our service advantage.

This encourages the buyer to rethink her strategy. This could be a case where saving money on the front end results in higher cost on the back end. Zero in on the risk factor. Ask which offers the greater risk—paying a little more than she anticipated or not getting what she needs to do the job she wants done.

Buying dissonance. There is a concept in psychology called "cognitive dissonance." Simply, this means people feel the need to act and think consonantly. If a person's behavior does not fit their thought process, the thinking will often shift to fit the behavior. If you can point to objective criteria in the buyer's needs, this may be enough to cause him to reconsider his purchasing habits. You're asking, "Is the quality (the service, support, availability, etc.) you're willing to pay for consistent with all of your needs?"

Reversal. When you reverse an objection, use the objection as the very reason why he should buy. He gives you the information you need to respond effectively to the objection. For example, if the long-term ownership costs of your product are lower than the competition yet the up-front acquisition price is higher, reverse the objection:

> Mr. Buyer, if cost is your primary concern, that's ex-
> actly why you should go with our package. When you
> examine the life cycle of our product and the economy
> in usage, we offer you greater long-term savings.

You demonstrated to the buyer that his reason for
hesitating is the very same reason that he should move
ahead. Convince him with his own argument. You can
reverse many objections this way; however, be cautious.
Any response that comes across as flippant or canned has
the opposite effect you want.

Trial Close. If you sense that the buyer is close to a decision
but needs some nudging, use the trial close. Ask the following two questions, which refocus him more positively on
the nonprice reasons why he wants to do business with
your company:

> Mr. Buyer, if you were to make a decision on any and
> all variables other than price, who would you go with
> and why?

At this point, let the buyer respond. Listen to his
answer for the number of nonprice issues. For the sake of
argument, let's assume the buyer responds with service,
quality, product availability, and support. He's giving you
four nonprice reasons for your second question:

> Mr. Buyer, doesn't it make more sense to go with us
> and get four out of the five things you want than to go
> with the competition and only get one of the five
> things you want, which is a cheaper price?

Using his priorities, you've built a strong case for
purchasing from your company.

Sell Loyalty. If your company has a long history of serving this customer well, remind him of everything you've done to make his life easier. Prove your case with documentation of special favors. Brag about everything above and beyond the call of duty that you have performed. Unless your salespeople blow your company's horn, no one will. Some buyers need a friendly reminder with a trip down memory lane to help them realign their thinking. If your company has excelled, you deserve credit for it.

Success Stories. Reassuring buyers with stories of others who have paid more to do business with your company is a good strategy. Some buyers respond favorably to knowing that they are not the only ones who pay more for your package. This is the "bandwagon" approach. Use proof sources such as testimonial letters to reinforce your position.

Another way to capitalize on success stories is to alert your salespeople for instances in the customer's business when he initially paid more for something and in the long run is glad he did. Use this twenty-twenty hindsight sales tool. Call attention to the previous value-added buying scenario and draw an analogy to the similarity of this situation.

Alternate Advantage Overload. Like the reversal, this method ironically uses price to justify itself. Use the higher price as a springboard for reintroducing other key benefits:

> Yes, Mr. Buyer, we are higher when it comes to price. We are also higher when it comes to service, quality, customer satisfaction, and delivery. We knew that we could be high in all those areas or low in all those areas so we chose the high ground. Shouldn't you?

Practice makes perfect. You want your salespeople to deliver this response with passion and conviction. Enthusiasm is contagious and your customers must test positive for your package.

Discretionary Funds. Businesses have budgets for just about everything, including discretionary items. Because these are nonspecific categories, less stringent requirements govern them. If the buyer likes an idea, she may pursue it with the knowledge that discretionary money is available. Pursuing this with buyers is another alternative to the price objection:

> Ms. Buyer, it's been my experience that most businesses have discretionary dollars available and will use them if convinced of the return value of an idea. Is that true in your organization, too?

The worst-case scenario is that the buyer will say no. It was certainly worth the effort.

VIP List, Three Questions, and Walk. At times, the last alternative is to give the buyer something to consider as you leave. After several responses to the price objection, leave the door open. Make it easy for the buyer to reverse his decision to use the cheaper alternative:

> Mr. Buyer, before you make your final decision, I would ask that you please take a few moments to review our Value In Purchasing list. Also, I would like to suggest that you ask yourself these three questions about the selection you'll make. If at that point you're not convinced that the other option meets your needs, we would be happy to work with you on the package we've discussed here today.

Naturally, the three questions spotlight your unique advantages, which coincidentally are the competition's weaknesses. A variation of this "three question" concept is to leave the buyer with three questions to ask your competitor about his package. These questions should reflect your company's depth of knowledge in your industry. If your questions stymie the competition, they expose his lack of depth. Provide your salesforce with a list of these questions and suggest they use them for those last-effort scenarios when they need a little extra help.

These strategies for handling price objections are a sampling of how your salespeople can respond to price resistance. Have your salespeople prepare three of these responses in their own wording. Instruct them to commit these ideas to memory. It builds their resilience and effectiveness in dealing with the most difficult objection they encounter: price!

NEGOTIATING

The selling skill that most people have been using since birth is negotiation. People learn at an early age that "give-and-take" is a fundamental human-relations dynamic. Is it any wonder that successful people are strong negotiators? The goal of value-added negotiating is to arrive at a win/win outcome. What possible gain is there for a salesperson who negotiates a win/lose or lose/win scenario? The first thing to teach your salespeople is the principle of equity.

Everyone likes to win. Everyone wants to feel that he or she is treated equitably by others. It's important in sales to *give* as good as one *gets*. The mutual win philosophy motivates people to accept a we-oriented solution. And "we" is a lot stronger than "me." When your salespeople acknowledge the buyer's desired outcome and actively work toward it, they engender a spirit of cooperation that helps them achieve their negotiating objectives.

The following ideas help your salespeople become stronger, we-oriented, value-added negotiators.

Time

Instruct your salespeople to use time prudently. Most salespeople have the word *Hungry* emblazoned on their foreheads. And buyers know this. In the heat of the moment, salespeople make concessions that under different circumstances they wouldn't normally make. Prudently dragging their feet is a negotiating fundamental that your people must use to create an equitable settlement. This goes against everything they've ever heard about sales: "Strike while the iron is hot!"

Sharp buyers understand the dynamics of time and how to use it to their advantage. Astute salespeople are less likely to be duped by the customer's projected sense of urgency. Train your staff to understand time. Teach them to avoid projecting a sense of urgency that equates to desperation. What your salespeople negotiate is related directly to how hungry they appear to buyers.

Another way to use time to your advantage relates to the open-endedness of the offer. Open-ended "deals" do not motivate buyers to act. If your group makes concessions, set a time limit for the buyer's taking advantage of it. Make a huge deal out of the concession. Advise the buyer it's an unusual concession and unlikely to recur in the future. Be careful not to establish buying precedents that encourage future concessions. Deadlines reinforce the uniqueness of this action.

Salespeople have deluded themselves for years into believing that "one more call" will make the critical difference in the sale. At that point, they become prisoners of hope in certain accounts. They believe that a few more calls will do the trick. It's difficult for managers to get salespeople to let go of an account that keeps them hostage with dubious promises. It's also in the buyer's best interest to keep a few vendors hanging in case a primary supplier drops the ball. So what's the point?

Buyers are like salespeople in this respect. The more time you can get buyers to spend evaluating, testing, and retesting your concept the more committed they are to it. Get buyers to spend time with your salespeople. This builds a sense of commitment to your solution while limiting the amount of time they can spend with the competition.

Timing is everything. Your people either use it or abuse it. In negotiating, there is no room for misusing it. Help your staff understand this message. Teach them to embrace it as a friend.

Price

We have invested a great deal of time and ink in this book discussing the issue of price in sales. And yet, it is only one buying criterion. Freud likened the personality to an iceberg. He said that the tip of the iceberg is the conscious mind. The rest of the mind, the unconscious, is beneath the surface. This is where the real action is.

This holds true for price. It's only the tip of the iceberg. It's the most visible portion of the buyer's needs because he positions it that way. Charge your salespeople to expose "beneath-the-surface" issues that mitigate price as the sole buying criterion. During negotiations, your salespeople must keep nonprice issues on the table. Shine a million-watt spotlight on these other buying criteria. It's the buyer's role to minimize them and the seller's role to maximize them.

When confronting the price issue, use the gravity principle. It's a lot easier to go down than to bring it back up. One caveat: If you must negotiate price, start high and work your way down. Once the price is lowered, it's very difficult to raise it again. Before lowering your price ask yourself these questions:

- Can we add value instead of cut price?
- Can this be sold more profitably somewhere else?
- How much pressure is this customer experiencing?
- How much profit will we make?

- Are we on an irreversible precedent-setting course?
- Does it start a bigger price war?
- Will our trust bond be broken?
- Does discounting this piece of business fit our overall strategic plan?
- Are there nonprofit-oriented reasons why we want this business—e.g., Hi-Visibility account/Hi-Prestige account?
- Will we resent the business after accepting it?
- Will this be a high-aggravation account?
- What is the client potential?
- Can we afford to invest valuable resources in this type of account?
- What do I risk by not discounting?
- How will we say no? (With a higher than average bid? By withdrawing our bid? By being late with our bid?)

Risk

Risk is a funny business. Most people live more risk daily than they realize but choose to ignore it. Crossing the street, flying in an airplane, and giving someone your heart all involve risk. Most people do not think about it that way. These are normal parts of living. Risk is a normal part of negotiating. Ironically, many find this an uneasy yet familiar concept.

George Meany, the great labor negotiator, once said, "Never sit down to a negotiating table unless you're willing to stand up." Every negotiation involves risk. Failing to negotiate or not negotiating the best win/win outcome presents an even greater risk. Explain the risk factors to your group. Help them deal with the uneasiness of risk. Give them the information and skills they need to minimize the impact of risk on the negotiation. Doing anything involves risk. Doing nothing is also a risk. With the former, your group controls the risk. With the latter, they submit to it.

Areas of Flexibility

When the rubber meets the road, your group may need to make some concessions. Assuming they have already asked the fundamental question—"Can we add value instead of cutting price?"—their choices turn to other areas. Anticipating which concessions are acceptable and which are not results in a more equitable outcome. Study and experiment with the following areas of flexibility before your salespeople ever get to the table.

• *Funny money* is an area of flexibility. Funny money is anything you concede that has a real dollar value for the customer substantially higher than your cost. You realize the full impact value on the customer while incurring only a fraction of the cost. For example, extended warranties may offer the customer hundreds of dollars in savings, but your cost may be thirty cents on the dollar. You give one dollar in perceived value and spend only thirty cents for it. Other examples include: extended terms, free shipping, samples, preventive maintenance programs, etc. Prepare your salespeople in advance by equipping them with a list of funny-money alternatives.

• *Volume concessions* invite two schools of thought. One espouses volume commitments from customers for any concession that you make. If you cut the price, get the buyer to purchase more product. The other school of thought believes the opposite. If it's not a good deal for your company at this price level, why should you sell more of it at the lower price? You figure it out!

• *Future discounts* maintain the integrity of your current price levels while offering the customer a future opportunity to save as he continues to purchase in higher volumes. Rebates and frequent-buyer programs are variations of this concept. Issue partial credits for goods purchased to be used in the future for additional purchases. The customer gets real dollar savings, and you do it with funny money.

• *Raise prices* in other areas. Consider this option. If the customer squeezes you for a cheaper price because he increases usage in one area, take his logic full circle. Raise prices in those areas where he decreases usage. Isn't that a consistent philosophy? You may encounter some resistance to this concept but it's certainly worth the effort. He may concede that it's a relevant issue—especially if he benefits overall.

These areas of flexibility increase your negotiating leverage. When your salesforce enters a negotiation equipped with flexibility, it enhances their position. Encourage them to concede prudently and selectively. Random concessions create a feeding frenzy for customers and encourage nibbling. Nibbling is like being bitten to death by a duck. Nibblers take a bite at a time until they've extracted a full-course meal of concessions. Warn your salespeople to exercise caution with this type.

Also, there is a rule in negotiation that states, "He who caves in first gives more than half his share." If you concede first, you will go more than halfway. Encourage customers to offer the first split. After prudently dragging your feet, counter with your offer. The outcome will pleasantly surprise you. Don't split first!

Negotiating has existed since Adam and Eve discussed apples in the Garden of Eden. Negotiating intimidates a lot of people, and they respond with anxiety. Some try to avoid it altogether because it's confrontation. Nobody invented the rules of negotiation. They're timeless. Negotiating is one of our first experiences of working things out with other people. Those who benefit from negotiations advocate a double-win scenario, actively work toward that outcome, and understand the dynamics of negotiation. You either pay or play. It's that simple.

CHAPTER SUMMARY

Objections are a reality for salespeople. Price objections are a probability for every salesperson. Those who anticipate and proact to them enjoy a greater likelihood of success. Persistence and preparation go a long way toward helping your staff. Teach them to persist within a customer-oriented environment. Explain that anticipation coupled with preparation does not create objections. Have them prepare three powerful rebuttals to price objections using the ideas in this chapter.

5
Value-Added
Customer Service

Have you hugged your customer lately?
Have you told 'em that you care?
Have you reached out boldly . . .
And said, "We know you're there"?

What have you said?
What have you done?
How have you hugged 'em
And said, "You're number one"?

In a crazy, mixed-up, me-first world
Where greed is the game to play,
Have you hugged your customer lately
And said, "In our book you're OK"?

When the well is dry,
And your hopes are low,
And your business has gone to pot . . .
You don't have to look far
Just beyond your nose
'Cause you've hugged your customer not.

Have you taken 'em for granted,
Expecting to rule the roost?
Or have you hugged 'em fondly
And given your sales a boost?

I'm a hugger, a plugger, and a big-league slugger
Because I follow this simple rule.
If I want to succeed and make my mark
I just live like a huggin' fool.

Tom Reilly

I spoke on Tuesday in Appleton, Wisconsin, at a sales rally. When I finished my presentation, I packaged my cassette tapes and books to prepare them for overnight shipment. I would speak on Friday at a rally in Milwaukee and wanted to sell the tapes after the presentation. Over the years I've learned to make it painless for hotels to ship things for you. Therefore, I prepared everything for shipment.

I handed the boxes to the desk clerk, explained the urgency that they ship the next day, and received her commitment that she would personally handle it for me. I slept well that Tuesday evening knowing that my packages would arrive Thursday morning in plenty of time for the Friday rally.

When I arrived Thursday evening at the Milwaukee hotel, I immediately checked for my packages. They weren't there. When I called the overnight shipping company, they informed me that the packages had not shipped until Thursday—not Wednesday as I had instructed the clerk and she had promised. I called the Appleton hotel and guess who answered the phone? The desk clerk who agreed to ship the boxes on Wednesday morning. I explained who I was.

"Oh yes, Mr. Reilly. You're the tape man. I shipped your tapes just like you wanted."

"When did they go?" I asked.

"Wednesday morning. Just the way you requested."

I responded, "I'm really confused. The overnight shipper informed me that the boxes didn't ship until today and they have your signature on a shipping invoice."

"Sir," she said coldly, "you'll need to talk to my supervisor. She'll be in tomorrow morning." Click. She hung up on me.

I was livid. Not only did she fail to perform a simple task; she lied to cover it up and then had the audacity to hang up on me. I didn't sleep well that night. All I could think about was how much money I would lose in tape sales because a clerk failed to perform her job.

The next morning I called the Appleton hotel and reached the supervisor. I ranted and raved. "How does something this incredibly stupid happen? I made it painless for the clerk. All she had to do on Wednesday was give the shipping-company driver the boxes."

She repeatedly asked, "And then what happened? And what else? And what will happen to your tape sales now?"

The whole time I was blustering she was listening to my words and my tone of voice. At the precise strategic moment, she said, "You're right. We really blew it. And if I were you, I would be even more angry than you are. You have every right to be mad at us. Can we please pay your shipping charges and compensate you for your stay at our hotel?"

I was flabbergasted. Here was a front-desk supervisor admitting that they were human and had made a mistake, giving me "permission" to be mad at them, apologizing, and trying to compensate me for my inconvenience.

"No," I drawled. "The shipper agreed to have the tapes here before the first break, and I've made arrangements to have someone set them up in the hallway outside the meeting room. It will be OK. I was just wondering how this could happen."

Again she said, "You're right, Mr. Reilly, we blew it. . . . "

How did I go from absolute frustration to acquiescence? The supervisor understood the principles of solid customer relations. She actively listened to the situation while giving me an opportunity to vent my frustration. She acknowledged my right to be angry and nondefensively accepted responsibility for the problem. Once she diffused the emotion, she offered a compensation solution. Frankly, her concern and contrition caught me off guard.

This scenario could have gone either way. When I perform this "Think of the last time you got really bad service" exercise in my customer-service seminars, there are numerous stories that go in the other direction. There are always frustrated and alienated consumers in my programs relating horror stories of companies and employees who failed to try to make a bad situation better. It's sad but true.

And it's always the small things that people talk about in the seminars: being ignored by clerks, wrong orders in restaurants, condescending attitudes by salespeople, being perceived as an interruption by employees, a cracked coffee cup, no towels in a hotel room, being put on hold on the phone forever, operators answering the phone with an edge in their voice, bureaucratic policies that make no sense, salesclerks who fail to thank customers, unempowered employees who can't and won't make decisions, postal workers who move at a snail's pace, overcharging and underdelivering, and supervisors who fail to rectify the mistakes their people make.

In customer relations, it's axiomatic that the same things that frustrate and alienate us also frustrate and alienate our customers. Whatever makes you angry makes your customer angry. People identify with that concept. They remember being treated badly and can appreciate how their customers feel when they're treated the same way.

In spite of the service-awareness explosion in this country, the proliferation of books on the topic, and the lip service paid to it by most companies, we still have a long way to go with service. With products becoming increasingly similar, markets maturing, and profit margins eroding, companies must look to service as a differentiation strategy. Improving customer service is the quickest, least expensive, and most highly visible competitive strategy your company can employ. One reason is the simplicity of customer service. It's people helping people get more of what they want. It's business systems that make it easy for customers to buy. It's management's awareness and acceptance that Total Quality Management includes quality of products *and* service.

UNIVERSAL RULES OF BUSINESS

These rules are fundamental to all businesses and a starting point for improving customer-service.

Rule #1: Everyone in the organization is a salesperson. Everyone sells something to someone. This is one of the oldest clichés in business and it's true. Management sells change to employees. Employees sell ideas to management. Peers sell programs to each other. Salespeople sell products to customers. Anytime someone in the organization attempts to persuade another person, he's selling—even if it's an intangible idea.

Rule #2: Not everyone believes rule number one. In fact, many people are insulted during my customer-service seminars when I assert that they are salespeople. They deny, argue, and rebuff. Much of their resistance comes from the traditional prejudices against salespeople. Less-argumentative participants pay lip service to this concept. And a few may embrace it. What's certain is that it is not universally accepted or practiced as gospel.

Rule #3: Everyone has a customer. Traditional customers are external. Internal customers are those within the organization whom other employees serve. Data processing serves many other departments. Those departments are their internal customers. Human resources often serves every other department. Those departments are their internal customers. The credit department is the internal customer for the salesforce, and so on. Most corporate settings are so interwoven that everyone is serving each other. Not a bad concept, eh? Everyone in the organization treating everyone else with the respect generally reserved for external customers.

Rule number three has two corollaries. First, you can only serve your external customers to the degree to which you serve your internal customers. Second, everything you do to serve your internal customers has an outward rippling effect on your external customers. Simply, external customers directly or indirectly experience how employees treat each other. Customer satisfaction mirrors employee satisfaction.

The fundamental question for organizations that want to improve service quality is, "Who are your customers and how can you serve them better?" The answer is your customer-service policy.

WHAT IS CUSTOMER SERVICE?

When I ask this question in seminars, I hear things like "The customer has a problem and we solve it," "The customer has a question and we answer it," and "When the customer calls, we deal with it." Reactivity underlies each answer. The customer does something that causes you to act. The assumption is that unless there's a problem, question, or inquiry the customer does not get service: no problem, no service.

In many companies, customer service is *not* a philosophy. It's a department or group of people who are responsible for handling customers: people handlers.

Customer service is a philosophy of doing business in which all employees *feel* and *act* accountable for customer satisfaction. It's not a fad—rather it's an operating philosophy for the organization. All employees must feel responsible for creating satisfied customers and actively work toward that goal.

Much of customer service goes unnoticed because it is proactive. Employees take the initiative to nip problems in the bud. Management empowers employees to make decisions, instructs them to do it right the first time, and encourages a mindset of continuous improvement. When employees internalize this sense of mission, serving becomes as natural as breathing. People begin looking for ways to "get better" for customers.

Employees who commit to this philosophy understand that you're either adding value or cost to the organization. If you look for ways to deliver better service, you're adding value. If you're reactive, waiting for the customer to inspire you to get better, you're a cost center. And there's no job security as a cost center. Proactive, value-adding employees who serve customers understand that the customer is revenue and that non-service-delivering employees are overhead. Lip service to this philosophy is insufficient. The employee's effort must be dynamic and consistent. Anything less is cosmetic.

WHAT IS CUSTOMER SATISFACTION?

It's such a simple question that it lures you into reciting manifestations of customer service: repeat business, customers smile and say thanks, word-of-mouth advertising, the buyer feels good, fewer objections and complaints, etc. All of these are examples of satisfied customers. However, customer satisfaction is a simple concept. It's the relationship between your performance and the customer's expectations. If you exceed his expectations, you have a satisfied customer. If you underperform his expectations, you have a dissatisfied customer.

When employees understand that customer satisfaction is a performance-based concept, creating it is much easier. Behavioralizing this philosophy means always working to exceed the customer's expectations. The critical element is the customer's perception. It's always his perception that counts. Whether or not you deliver great service is not the issue. The issue is whether or not the customer perceives that you deliver great service. This relates to the concept I discussed earlier in this book, *perceived value.*

Buyers want service. Two-thirds of the business you lose from your back door is because of vendor indifference. And it costs the average company five to six times more money to get a new customer than to keep an existing one happy. Creating satisfied customers is a double win. It requires less effort and money on your part and the customers love it.

Additionally, satisfaction is contagious. When employees actively work to create satisfied customers, often times customers reciprocate with a "thank-you." Genuine appreciation from customers boosts morale. This in turn has a dramatic impact on job satisfaction that affects future performance. Customer satisfaction is a two-way street. Everyone benefits. Management. Customers. Employees. What a great formula for success!

SO WHY DON'T COMPANIES DO IT?

If customer satisfaction makes dollars and sense, why don't more companies create it? Good question. Here are the four most common reasons. First, money. Some believe it's too expensive to initiate a customer-service program. They misunderstand its simplicity. For them, it means systems, equipment, and additional personnel. In reality, it requires a philosophical commitment by everyone. The behaviors are free.

Second, time. Research indicates that it takes more than twice as long to sell to a new prospect than an existing customer. Yet, some misconceive that it's time-intensive to service existing customers. This excuse surfaces time and again in seminars. "We're swamped. We're overworked. We're doing well just to answer the phones. We don't have time to slow down for every caller to hold his hand. I'm only one person—what can I do?" These remarks are more common than you might think. Think of the last time your phone rang while you were working on something. Did you think if they would just leave you alone, you could get your job done?

Third, lack of skills. "No one ever taught me how to deliver better customer service." Again, this is a misunderstanding of the philosophical roots of customer service. It's an attitude or mindset. When one accepts that, the behaviors flow naturally from the attitude. The skills of customer service are simple acts of consideration—the manifestation of the Golden Rule. Treat your customers the way you wish they would treat you.

Fourth, apathy. For some, success breeds complacency. Companies get busy, they grow, their profits soar, they forget how eager they were to serve, and they develop the attitude that the customer needs them more than they need the customer. They casually send messages like, "We may not be the only company in town, but we'll sure act like it." They begin to believe that they're invincible and shortly discover how vulnerable they are.

DANGER SIGNALS

If any of the above sound like your company, be careful. You may not be delivering the type of value-added service needed to compete in today's market. Recognizing and accepting that your company lacks a competitive service philosophy is the first step in recovering. The following danger signals will help you determine if your company needs help.

Internal Signals

Certain things, inside your organization, signal trouble. For instance, when you start believing your own PR about how great you are and let it go to your head. You've crossed the line from pride to arrogance. I've seen this a number of times with really good companies. They begin with a passion for leading their industries. From there, they excel against performance standards. Pride develops. The good ones remember how tough the journey was. The really bad ones forget the climb to the top and become pompous.

This feeds another internal signal: perceiving the customer as an aggravation rather than an opportunity—a pain versus a gain. Then, you treat the customer as an interruption.

The following quiz helps you determine if you're "hugging your customers."

- Do you view the customers' questions and visits as interruptions?
- Are you difficult for customers to personally contact?
- Do you ask customers routinely, "How are we performing for you?"
- Do your employees/peers like your customers?
- Do you feel it's too costly to hug your customers?
- Do you thank every customer for his/her business?
- Have you ever said, "We're the only game in town—we don't need to hug"?
- Is it as important to hug customers in good times as well as in bad times?

- Will you open a closed store to help a customer?
- Do you get all of the repeat business you should get?
- Have you said, "If they (customers) would just leave me alone, I could get my job done"?
- Is customer satisfaction a guiding principle in your business?

External Signals

Customers warn you that you're not delivering the service they want and need. You notice less repeat business—the customer doesn't call back as much anymore. You receive more customer complaints—especially about wrong shipments, quality problems, and price objections. The customer mistakenly calls you and orders with your competitor's catalog numbers. You have less referral business because customers aren't giving your name to their friends. Those perceived interruptions that annoyed you are now going to your competitors. They love these "interruptions."

WHAT CAN MANAGEMENT DO?

This is a top-down process. Customer-oriented organizations begin with the culture. Culture building starts with a vision. Managers communicate the urgency of this vision—they plan, strategize, and act. Get the MOST out of your efforts:

- Mission—communicate your mission (your vision) and seek employee buy-in.
- Objectives—set objectives that support the mission.
- Strategies—develop strategies that help achieve the objectives.
- Tactics—design field-level tactics that support the overall strategy.

The employees must witness your passion. They must perceive that creating customer satisfaction is the dominant goal of the organization. This begins at the top. Do you pay yourselves bonuses on gross sales or customer satisfaction? How often do you get out in the field? Are you accessible to customers or do you hide? Do you speak often about the importance of customer service? What are you doing today to create an allied army of satisfied customers to help you wage war on the competition?

Customer satisfaction mirrors employee satisfaction. To create satisfied customers, managers must work on employee satisfaction. Employee involvement, participation, and empowerment boost morale and subsequently performance. Job enrichment increases satisfaction. Employees who feel they're being treated equitably are more satisfied with their jobs. It's easier for them to give their best when they feel they're getting your best in return.

Managers contribute to customer satisfaction when they go to Mach 1 response time: response time at the speed of sound. By identifying barriers to effective customer service and eliminating these obstacles, managers increase the speed with which employees can respond. Determining the source of these obstacles is as simple as asking customers and employees, "What gets in the way of world-class service?"

A key barrier is *employee powerlessness*. Empower your employees to make decisions and give them the wherewithal to enact them. Encourage them to proact—to nip it in the bud. When they see a problem and correct it on their own, reward their initiative.

Helping employees articulate their service philosophy is another way to shape the culture. Construct a customer's Bill of Rights. Hold a staff meeting and ask the group this question: "What do our customers have a right to expect when they come to us for business?" Listen to *their* responses. Let *them* compile a list of *their* ideas. This is the

Bill of Rights. Have it printed for distribution. Turn it into a poster for the office. Sign it "The employees of . . . "

The following Bill of Rights was constructed by a small company in St. Louis. Its simplicity is brilliant.

Customer Bill of Rights

Our Customers have a right to expect . . .
- A fair price for the goods and services we sell;
- For us to go the extra mile every time they call;
- Accuracy in shipping and billing;
- A pleasant atmosphere with knowledgeable people and no hassles;
- Ready availability of top quality products;
- To be treated with respect and courtesy.

                    (Signed, the employees of . . .)

I couldn't have written it better myself. How would you like to do business with this company? Imagine how difficult it must be to compete with this company. Imagine how much fun it must be to work for this company. Imagine how motivating it could be to manage these employees. These are decent people treating customers with respect.

WHAT CAN EMPLOYEES DO?

Since this is a shared responsibility between management and employees, both must actively work to create satisfied customers. It begins for employees when they understand and accept their role in creating satisfied and loyal customers. Then they are more likely to assume responsibility for customer satisfaction. When employees adopt the customer-service attitude, the behavior follows. It naturally flows. This behavior generally falls into two categories: front-line and behind-the-scenes activities.

Front-Line Activities

These are things employees do when eyeball-to-eyeball with the customer. The most rudimentary thing employees need to understand and accept is that perceiving is believing, and it's always the customer's perception that counts. Again, whether or not your company delivers great service is not the issue. The real issue is whether the customer *perceives* it that way. When employees buy into this concept, they understand the goal more clearly.

One front-line activity is naive listening. I heard this term a long time ago and wish I could credit the author. It means to listen as a child listens to a story: intent, interested, and involved in the story. Listening naively to the customer means reserving judgment. Listen for everything that is said and unsaid. Look for the nonverbals. What is the customer saying between the lines? When the customer is unloading, absorb it all while remaining nondefensive. When the customer speaks, he vents, and you get valuable information to satisfy him.

Another front-line activity is follow-up . . . the number-one weakness for most salespeople. Calling the customer back with information on a timely basis automatically differentiates your company. Following up after the sale, especially when there is no potential for additional orders, is good business and a radical concept for most people. How would you feel if the last car salesperson you bought from called you one year after the sale to see how things were going? My guess is you would be shocked (in a very positive way). Teach your employees to use follow-up as a positioning strategy while ensuring customer satisfaction.

Living the philosophy of "Promise a lot and deliver more" is a simple way for employees to understand how they personally affect customer satisfaction. With this mindset firmly rooted, they know that exceeding buyer expectations is how a company earns the moniker of a customer-driven organization. The behavior is simple. Always look for ways to go beyond the customer's expectations.

Projecting the "attitude of gratitude" makes customers feel welcomed. It's being grateful for the opportunity to serve. Consider this. On the front end, you sold the buyer on the concept that if there were ever a problem after the sale you would handle it promptly. This is the moment of truth. It's time to deliver on the promises you made to get the business. The message he hears when your employees answer the phone differentiates your company. It's either "We're excited you called and we're ready to serve," or "I was busy when you called so let's see how quickly we can dispose of this. I need to get back to my real job." With the former, he feels like a welcomed visitor. The latter feels like the "bum's rush."

Behind-the-Scenes Activities

These are things your employees do, many times without recognition, that result in better service. Developing a philosophy of doing things right the first time every time is a work ethic that customers appreciate. It goes unnoticed because you're creating *the absence of mistakes*. It's built on a simple time-management principle that if you don't have time to do it correctly the first time, when would you have time to do it over again? Doing things correctly the first time is a time and money saver. Mistakes cost. Doing things repeatedly until they are correct is a cost many organizations cannot incur. I got the following from my printer.

Being proactive is never having to say you're sorry. When an employee fixes something that would later sur-

---

Is Quality Important?

Quality printing (thx kind wx do) is a dxlicatx procxss. And wx takx thx quality of our printing vxry sxriously. Wx hatx mistakxs. Xspxcially, onxs that happxn ovxr and ovxr again. Any kind of mistakx, big or small, is a pain to dxal with. And wx think onx is too many, bxcausx onx flaw rxpxatxd ovxr and ovxr makxs you look bad. That's why wx intxntionally altxrxd this mxssagx to show you how xvxn thx smallxst mistakxs can grow into an xxtrxmxly largx problxm.

But, if mistakes are corrected before they happen, you'll get a finished product that's easy on the eyes and conveys the image you want it to. We think that's what quality printing is all about.

---

face as an issue for the customer, he is proacting. There's no apology needed for delivering quality products wrapped in a bundle of quality services. Seeing what needs to be done and doing it before it becomes an issue is the heart and soul of value-added selling.

TIPS FOR HUGGING YOUR CUSTOMER

This list of ideas is as homegrown as you can get. It comes from the rank and file of those who deliver service daily—employees who have attended my customer-service programs. They all responded to the question, "How can you deliver better customer service in your job?" These are their ideas, not mine.

1. Smile more often at my customers.
2. Project a more professional and personal attitude.
3. Greet my customers with a handshake and warm welcome.

4. Get more knowledgeable.
5. Call back on a timely basis.
6. Be accurate in my paperwork.
7. Have an optimistic attitude when dealing with people.
8. Use direct eye contact.
9. Be a patient listener.
10. Demonstrate concern for the customer above and beyond his or her business.
11. Give the customer my undivided attention.
12. Keep the customer informed of all information relevant to his or her business.
13. Use sincere compliments and appreciation.
14. Let the customer know how I'm following up; don't leave the customer hanging.
15. Demonstrate respect and concern for the customer.
16. Speak calmly—especially when the customer is upset.
17. Say thank you as often as I can.
18. Don't put anyone on hold longer than two minutes without getting back to him or her.
19. Use the customer's name often.
20. Get to know the customer as a person.
21. Ask what I can do to make the customer's life easier.
22. Work with my peers to help them serve customers better.

These twenty-two ideas are brilliant. They read like a primer for great customer relations. These are very special because the people who wrote them believe them and are living them every day.

CHAPTER SUMMARY

In this chapter, we focused on the importance of supporting your outside sales efforts with inside customer service. An easy conclusion is that it's the inside staff's job to create customer satisfaction. Wrong! It's everyone's responsibility—inside and outside. Your salespeople affect customer satisfaction with their performance and their promises. How employees treat each other also affects customer satisfaction. Managers who treat employees with respect and empower them to make decisions build a solid foundation with stones of excellence and equity. Employees stand on them to support customers. It's a great place to build customer loyalty.

6
Key Dynamics
of Sales Management

All of the sales training dollars in the world have minimal impact on an organization without the full support of management. The saying "If it's to be, it's up to me!" has special meaning for organizations attempting to create a sales and marketing culture.

Tom Reilly management seminar

I recently heard a professor of Soviet studies from Princeton University offer his perspective on the coup that reshaped the Soviet Union and ended the Cold War. He was contrasting the U.S. system to the Soviet system of government. He described the long and oppressive history the Soviets had with strong leaders. Their system was built around a person. On the other hand, the United States has a long, rich history of a leadership system. Our success is built on a system—their failure on a leader-dependent culture.

What a great analogy for companies! Over the years, I've noticed that the strongest companies with whom I've worked have strong systems in place that continue to guide people after specific leaders are long gone. The most prudent business strategy for any company is to develop a strong leadership system that supports the value-added sales philosophy. The best-case scenario is strong leaders operating in a strong leadership system.

This chapter focuses on the six critical dynamics of a strong sales management system. Each is a necessary ingredient in the recipe for sales managers' success. The dynamics appear in a rough order of implementation. I begin with *selection*—hiring the right person. From there, I examine *training and developing* the person just hired. Then, I offer some ideas on how to set reasonable standards of performance: *goals* and objectives. Next, I suggest how sales managers can use *focusing* to help salespeople concentrate on high-priority activities and accounts. The next topic is *feedback* strategies. I finish the chapter with some ideas on *compensation*.

Each of these topics could be the subject of a separate book, and in most cases is. The purpose of this chapter is to spotlight these topics and challenge you to enhance your sales management system in each of these areas.

SELECTION

It all begins with the right person. After training tens of thousands of salespeople during the past eleven years, I still believe that you can teach professional selling to most people. I also accept that doing this is easier with some people than others. Starting with the right person cuts down on the learning curve. You reach break-even a lot quicker with the right person. Who is this right person I keep talking about? That's what this section is all about.

The cost of hiring and training a salesperson hovers around $15,000. That's a lot of money to throw away on underplanned and unstructured selection efforts. An even greater impact of hiring the wrong person is having that individual alienate valuable customers. One reason that sales managers fail to perfect their selection process is that they do it infrequently. They've forgotten one of the first rules they learned as rookie salespeople: prospect continuously.

You must have your line in the water continuously looking for new salespeople. Be proactive. Even if there is no immediate need, ongoing prospecting for candidates offers several benefits. When you place a blind ad in the paper, you may get a résumé from one of your own people—a dissatisfied employee. As you interview candidates, you hear industry news from competitive salespeople. Another benefit is that you compare your salesforce with talent that's available. An additional benefit is the indirect effect it has on your salesforce. If they know you're always looking for new talent, it encourages them to stay out of comfort zones.

If you have an ongoing selection effort with several highly qualified candidates, imagine how quickly you can fill a vacancy. Your region may never skip a beat. Contrast this to not interviewing, feeling desperate to fill a position, and making the wrong decision. You may need to terminate your new employee and begin the search again. Practice the same logic you've encouraged your salespeople to use: prospect often. And do it as scientifically as the process allows.

Whom Should You Hire?

For years industrial psychologists have toiled over the ideal profile for salespeople. Usually the profile looks more like superman than reality, but you can use their methods to narrow the field. Systematize your search and perfect it. Each time you use it, you get closer, sooner, to the target. Realize that there is no foolproof prediction method.

There will always be salespeople who break the model. The good news is that there are fewer of them. Companies that treat selection systematically have minimal problems compared to those who casually approach this topic.

Since you're compiling a list of desirable characteristics and this is a book on value-added sales management, remember that your goal is to hire someone who fits into the value-added sales culture. Do you want to hire someone who comes from an industry notorious for discounting or perceiving customers as necessary evils? Ask yourself this question: "Does this candidate's background contribute to our goals or impede our progress?" Background is no guarantee. You could have someone from the right background who didn't fit there and couldn't wait to get out. Also, you could have someone who got an inside look at the wrong background and decided to get out quickly. There is no rule of thumb here, but the question is worth considering.

Consider the job itself. Is this a sales job that requires heavy prospecting for new business and cold calling? Do you need someone who has strong offensive or defensive selling skills? This must surface during the interview. Some salespeople are fantastic at relationship selling and thrive in environments where they can "love a customer to death." Other salespeople prefer to operate as scouts—working hard to develop new pieces of business. For them, the challenge is the "hunt," not necessarily the "kill." Does your situation require a scout or a settler?

Do you want someone who is more product or sales oriented? What percent technical versus salesperson do you want? Fifty percent sales and 50 percent technical? How about 40 percent technical and 60 percent sales? What does your specific hiring situation require? If you have the technical support available to the salesforce, why do you need mostly technical ability? In your case, is it easier to teach the technical aspects of the position or the selling skills?

You're probably getting the idea that I have more questions than answers for this part of the book. You're right! This is the challenge of selecting the right person—answering the right questions. Within your experiences as a manager, you have the right answers. My questions elicit them.

What success have you enjoyed in the past going outside your industry? The profession of sales? Does it make sense to hire someone who already knows your industry? Do you want someone with an industry paradigm? It could make more sense to hire someone unscathed by the price sensitivity of your market. Someone who doesn't know or realize that companies can't sell value-added. Candidate naiveté might work to your advantage when hiring a value-added salesperson.

The same applies to nontraditional salespeople. This refers to hiring people who have come from jobs other than sales. What about teachers, technicians, customer-service personnel, human-resource employees, truck drivers, and firefighters? This list goes on. Do you have an inbreeding bias for salespeople that clouds your expectations? Review your company's experience when hiring these folks. Inbreeding also applies to hiring only salespeople from your organization. A problem with this philosophy is that these people bring the same corporate paradigms to the field as other reps.

I worked with a company that wanted only salespeople who grew up within their system. Their philosophy was simple: "When someone gets good enough on the inside, then we let him go into the field to be with our customers." The homegrown concept works well for a lot of companies. My question is, "How many really good people do they overlook along the way?" Having only one system for selection is dangerous. It presumes that good people do not live outside your perimeter.

Another consideration is where most of your successful people came from in the past. Did they respond to newspaper ads, send out résumés, come by word-of-mouth referrals, from competitive salesforces, or did they contact you directly while prospecting for a job? Replaying past successes has merit when hiring.

From all the questions I've suggested, list the characteristics you desire in a candidate. Look for these before, during, and after the interviews. Add the following characteristics to your list. I've observed these "success indicators" during eleven years of working with some of the best salespeople in this country.

• *Honesty*—Research indicates that the number one thing people look for in a salesperson is honesty and integrity. People like to do business with people they trust. Old-fashioned values never go out of style.

• *Initiative*—Self-starters require less day-to-day supervision and project the "extra miler's" philosophy in everything they do. They solve problems *before* they surface. They're proactive and have an internal kickstarter. They cold call and prospect without prompting. They ask questions and pursue answers on their own.

• *Internally controlled*—I discuss this concept more fully in Chapter 7. Internally controlled people feel that whatever happens in their lives results mostly from what they do or fail to do. They believe in and accept responsibility for most of what happens to them. These people understand that luck and fate are hollow concepts upon which to build a career.

• *Customer-oriented*—This concept has appeared in literature for decades variably as empathy, people-orientation, and concern for others. The construct is always the same. The value-added salesperson defines life in terms much bigger than herself. The sale is bigger than her commission. It's good business for her company and a needed solution for the customer.

• *Thorough*—Salespeople often scoff at attention to detail. They view it as trivial. How trivial is it to get the order correct the first time? How trivial is it to have the correct shipping information? And how trivial is it to have the correct pricing in a proposal? Consider the impact of typos and incorrect information on a résumé.

• *Follow-up*—According to buyers, the greatest weakness of salespeople in general is not delivering on promises or following up after the sale. How do you feel when someone fails to deliver on a promise?

• *Proactive*—This means taking the initiative—being a self-starter. Proactive salespeople anticipate and act.

• *Communications skills*—The ability to ask intelligent "pain-level-raising" questions, listen actively to the responses, and communicate a sales message that addresses those needs is critical to value-added selling. Support strategies like letter and proposal writing also require strong communication skills.

• *Organized*—Do you want someone who is organized or agonized? Disorganized salespeople require closer supervision. Because you micromanage them, it affects your time management. Do you have enough time to manage a poor self-manager?

• *Persistent*—In the chapter on handling price resistance, I discuss the importance of persistence. If a candidate does not persist in pursuing a sales job with your company, how aggressively will he pursue business for your company?

This list is a starting point. Combine it with your own ideas and look for these things during the selection process. At the end of this section, I include a postinterview Candidate Evaluation Questionnaire for you. It parallels this list of characteristics and gives you a scoring mechanism for assessing a candidate's strengths.

What Should You Ask During an Interview?

Every sales manager has favorite things to say and do during an interview. Today, in our litigious society, companies are becoming legally aware of what to ask. A simple rule of thumb prevails. When in doubt, don't—before you ask the human resources department or the legal department. That caveat behind us, let's examine what you *can* ask.

• *What do you expect from management?* You want to know if this person is a self-starter or if he wants management to do everything for him.

• *How often do you prospect and why?* If this is a new territory and the candidate has no cold calling experience, that's good information to know. If this candidate only prospects because he has been instructed to, that too is interesting.

• *How do you plan your day?* Are you curious how salespeople set priorities and schedule their time? You must know their method and reasoning.

• *What do you think customers want from salespeople?* This gives you insight into the candidate's understanding of the human factor in sales. It alerts you to how much thought this person gives to the relationship opportunity.

• *When you're on a roll, how do you keep yourself on a sales high?* This signals how insightful, creative, and internally controlled this person is. It also addresses the issue of resilience and his ability to handle defeat.

• *How does sales fit into your career path?* Is this a far-thinking person? Does this individual give much thought to his future or is he just looking for a job? Be cautious not to alienate or discourage career salespeople from sharing their desire to make selling a lifelong ambition. It's OK to want to be a career salesperson. Most people haven't got a clue what they want to do with the rest of their lives. Someone who wants to live in the trenches for his business career is not displaying a lack of leadership or ambition. He's expressing pride in his profession. Don't let your personal biases affect the answer to this question.

- *Would you describe your most successful sale?* It's interesting to determine if strategy or luck plays a role in someone's success. Luck may not surface as a label, but "being in the right place at the right time" is luck by anyone's definition. This question is important to determine if the person has a method for his success. Has he acquired the habit of success? Can he replicate it somewhere else?

- *How do you get new product ideas?* This tells you if the candidate is thinking about ways to help your company grow with new ideas in the future. It also says something about his openness to the customer's feedback. Generally, this is where all good ideas originate—at the source of the need.

- *What motivates you to win?* Over half the salespeople I train cannot tell me what motivates them. They don't understand their own internal motivation. How can you help this person when he cannot tell you which button is the hot one?

- *Would you walk me through your precall preparation?* Listen for the process and the content. If the candidate is surprised or taken off-guard by your question, she is accustomed to making calls—not sales.

- *Which selling skill is the most important?* You will probably hear the perfunctory response "Closing." Probe deeper. Determine how this person will sell your customers. Will the tone of the presentation be needs-driven or product-driven?

- *What type of customer is the hardest for you to sell?* Insight is critical for this response. Here, you're asking the salesperson to admit that he's human. Beware of macho denials like, "Nobody. I can sell anything to anybody."

Prepare your list of questions before the interview. When the candidate responds, give him plenty of room to answer. Accept the fact that he's probably nervous. Observe the nonverbals. Fifty-five percent of what we communicate is nonverbal. Read between the lines of what's not said. Challenge gaps on the résumé. Ask for testimonial letters from previous *customers.* Suggest that the salesperson prepare for you an employment proposal much like he might need to sell a customer. On it, he should list your needs and the benefits of his product. Have him return to present it formally. Finally, explain your value-added mission. Check his reaction to your company being in a price sensitive situation and having to sell value not price. Offer him an early price objection in terms of salary and watch him sell you on a higher one.

FIGURE 6
CANDIDATE EVALUATION QUESTIONNAIRE

1. Did references check out?   Yes _____   No _____
2. Does résumé reflect stability?   Yes _____   No _____
3. Are all time gaps accounted for on résumé? Yes _____   No _____
4. Does candidate have a record of success?   Yes _____   No _____
5. On a 1-10 scale, how did the candidate come across?
   (1 = Poorly, 10 = Great) _____

CHARACTERISTICS QUESTIONS

Honesty

Did the references substantiate this?   Yes _____   No _____

Did candidate use the word *honest* in the
interview to describe successful salespeople
or what buyers want?   Yes _____   No _____

Initiative

Did the candidate demonstrate initiative during the interview?	Yes ____	No ____
Did the candidate ask for a tour, request literature, or ask when he could start?	Yes ____	No ____

Internal Control

Did the candidate refer to luck in his quest for success?	Yes*____	No ____
Did his language indicate "he was in control" of his destiny?	Yes ____	No ____
Did the candidate blame the economy, poor product line, or lack of support for his failure?	Yes*____	No ____

Customer Orientation

Did the candidate discuss the importance of the customer?	Yes ____	No ____
Did he appear to be customer-oriented versus product-oriented?	Yes ____	No ____

Thorough

Were his questions thorough?	Yes ____	No ____
Was the candidate's résumé thorough?	Yes ____	No ____

Follow-Up

Did the candidate contact you after the interview?	Yes ____	No ____

Proactive

Did you get the impression that this candidate is proactive?	Yes ____	No ____

Communication Skills

Did the candidate listen well?	Yes ____	No ____
Was his eye contact steady?	Yes ____	No ____
Were his nonverbals open?	Yes ____	No ____
Were his questions thought-inspiring?	Yes ____	No ____

Organized

Was candidate prepared for the interview?	Yes ____	No ____
Does the candidate have a method for keeping himself organized?	Yes ____	No ____

Persistence

Did this candidate ask for the job?	Yes ____	No ____
Did he ask for the job more than once?	Yes ____	No ____

<u>Scoring</u>
Count the number of "yes" responses (except for the two asterisks). The more "yes" answers you receive, the better the candidate. Count a "no" response on the two questions with asterisks as a "yes" response for the total. The most a candidate can score is 25 (including the two "no" responses).

TRAINING AND DEVELOPMENT

If you think training is expensive, try not doing it! This is the oldest cliché in the human resources field. Trite and true. You've invested heavily in attracting the best talent you can afford. It makes sense to condition and position them for success. It's unreasonable to expect top performance from salespeople and not equip them with the skills to achieve that goal. Effective leaders constantly prepare their successors. You can't move on without having someone in the wings ready for the challenge.

Training and development is a mindset for growth-oriented cultures. The philosophy of *continuous improvement* applies to the individual also. In the first half of this book, I offered statistics demonstrating the importance of the salesperson to the sale. Those 35 to 37 percent numbers only apply to well-trained, knowledgeable employees. Your folks cannot deliver that much value without preparation.

Training Versus Development

Training prepares employees for specific job responsibilities. Development is less specific—it's "mind stretching" for the future. A well-rounded sales training program does both. There's an immediacy to meet today's training needs and a long-term strategy to prepare your salespeople for the future.

Today's professionals require technical and selling skills. To determine which skills your salespeople need, perform a job analysis. Scrutinize the demands of the job and list the necessary skills to perform the job according to standards. Evaluate your salespeople's performance in each of these areas. You're looking for a skills deficit. This gap becomes your training program.

Training Areas

There are three main areas in which you need to train your salespeople: company issues, product knowledge, and professional skills.

Company issues include things like paperwork systems, policies and procedures, facilities information, support services, etc. Product training includes everything you can do for your salespeople to boost their product knowledge and technical proficiency. A few years ago researchers discovered that 80 percent of the sales training dollars spent in this country went for product versus selling skills training. Is it any wonder that salespeople spend so much time talking about their products versus solutions for the customer? They've been trained (directly or indirectly) to think that way.

Professional skills include four skills sets: selling techniques, personal organizational skills, relationship skills, and motivational skills. You can further divide selling skills into Level I, fundamental skills, and Level II, advanced skills. Level I skills include:

- Market definition—determining where to call
- Sales letters—what to say and how to say it
- Getting appointments—what to say to the prospect on the phone
- Call preparation—routine procedures before calls
- Opening the call—how to establish rapport with customers
- Probing—the mechanics and content areas of questioning

- Presenting—how to deliver presentations with punch
- Closing—how to work out the details to create action
- Handling objections—being persistent without being a pest
- Following up—what to do in the postsale/no-sale phase

These are the most rudimentary things your salespeople need to know—the minimum of knowledge for sales success. Level II skills include more advanced topics that presume their knowing the fundamentals:

- Value-added selling—selling value not price
- Team selling—playing the coordinator role within the organization
- Account strategy—using planning skills to determine strategies and tactics
- Group selling—how to design and deliver powerful group presentations
- Selling concepts—how this differs from selling products

You can teach Level I and II skills together or independently. Some companies prefer to give the salesforce a chance to sell for a few months before teaching the more advanced material. The rationale is that the salespeople will appreciate it more after experiencing these needs firsthand.

Personal organization skills include time and territory management and goal setting. Relationship skills drive home the message that sales is a people business: identifying different buying styles and communication skills—listening and nonverbal communication. Motivational skills focus on how your salespeople keep themselves motivated, especially during times of stress, slumps, and rejection. The decision for when to teach these skills positions them as an important part of Level I training or Level II enhancements.

On the Job Training—OJT

Where to teach skills is a vital question that is part of an ongoing debate in human resources. Should we send a rookie into the field with an experienced rep to teach him the ropes? This approach has its merit and drawbacks.

A major drawback of OJT with experienced reps is that the lack of structure underprepares the trainee for systems knowledge—how all the pieces fit together. Another drawback is that the pro's mastery often intimidates the rookie, who may feel incapable of modeling this approach. This is especially true of "personality type" old pros who wield superpeople skills. A third major drawback is that the rookie may also learn the veteran's bad habits along with the good.

Proponents of this method vehemently argue the other point of view: The rookie sees real-life problems with realistic attempts at dealing with those problems. The trainee comes back to classroom training with tons of questions based on "real world" experiences. Another argument for this approach is that if you isolate specific "old pro" strengths to model then it's worth more live than even the best training video. The "bad habits" argument is downplayed by recommending an immediate debriefing after each field trip.

GOALS

Goals motivate. They direct one's efforts. Goals provide useful information on several fronts. Salespeople need objectives as a target and a feedback mechanism on their performance.

When setting goals, use these ideas to make them more achievable. Perhaps you've heard the old saying "Set SMART goals." These goals should be:

- Specific
- Measurable
- Achievable
- Realistic
- Timely

These help you set more challenging and motivating goals. Additionally, the following ideas add depth to your goal-setting efforts.

Time Horizon

The time frame for goals must allow for their successful completion. Few things are as demotivating and anxiety-producing as unrealistic deadlines. I've heard it said that there are no unrealistic goals—just unrealistic time frames. Build in a long- and short-term element to the goal. Long-term goals are where you want your staff to be ultimately. Short-term goals divide the long-term goal into smaller, manageable units that reinforce immediately. Long-term goals inspire . . . short-term goals guide.

Reinforcers

The cardinal rule for reinforcement is that the shorter the link between behavior and reinforcement the more powerful the reward. Schedule reinforcement for as soon as feasible after goal achievement. You'll get more bang for the buck. Also, the value of the reinforcer to the salesperson is critical to its effectiveness.

I consulted for a company in St. Louis on employee compensation. I was charged with conducting employee-attitude interviews on their current program to determine ways to improve it. The target group was telemarketers, ages fifty-five and older, all women, married to blue-collar workers. A key question I asked was, "If you were given a choice between a 10 percent dollar incentive for achieving sales quota this month or a three-day weekend that did not count toward your vacation, which would you prefer?" Without hesitation, they opted unanimously for the extra day off. It had high value to this group. In fact, one said to me, "Tom, if I had the chance for a three-day weekend, I wouldn't have the time to sit here and talk to you. I'd be out there now trying to figure out a way to meet quota!"

The boss ignored my prescriptions and decided to reward their performance with a three-hundred-dollar leather briefcase. My response was, "What are they going to do with it—wrap it around their bowling balls?" He paid me for my services and said good-bye. He violated the first rule in rewarding behavior: Make sure the reward is valuable to the other person.

Perceived Barriers

Barrier analysis prevents barrier paralysis. A key discovery from research on motivation theory is that perceived barriers inhibit performance. A question people consider before deciding to act is, "What obstacles do I face?" This is not always a conscious question. People consider this on an unconscious level also. Anticipating these barriers, developing contingency plans, and proacting can minimize the impact they have on your staff's enthusiasm.

Activity/Productivity Goals

Activity goals stress action: number of calls, calls to close, thirty minutes of professional reading each day, etc. They describe action steps or the process. Productivity goals focus on results: sales made, quota achievement, reaching profit goals, etc. Activity goals separate behavior into manageable units. These are bite-size chunks of actions that lead to the bigger goals. Activity goals are the quickest way to change behavior. When you emphasize production issues too early, you create goal anxiety. When you emphasize activity goals, you're stressing the process of success . . . something over which the person has greater control.

Initially, reinforce the effort not the results. As the behavior parallels the process, switch your focus to results. As a manager, this is one of the most difficult concepts to accept. You've been taught to believe in results-oriented behavior. This "reinforce-the-effort" philosophy flies in the face of everything you've heard about achievement. In the beginning, trying is good enough. Experiment with this concept and enjoy the results.

Involvement

Participation lowers resistance to change. The more you involve your salespeople in the goal-setting process the greater their commitment. Time and again, studies demonstrate that salespeople who set their own goals consistently set higher standards than management sets for them. Involve them, get their input, have them describe their action plan in detail, and reinforce their commitment.

In a book on value-added selling, a section on goal setting is incomplete without a reference to profit. When you establish goals, structure them to reflect margins as well as gross revenue. Select three Jumbo CD accounts and discuss objectives for these customers. Set goals that focus on offensive selling, defensive selling, and account retention. Use goals to reinforce your value-added sales management efforts.

FOCUSING

You've hired the right person, provided a solid foundation of training, and jointly set achievable and motivating goals. Now the challenge is to keep your salespeople focused on success. *Focusing is concentrating your efforts with a laser-beam intensity on achieving your value-added sales goals.* This applies to accounts and projects. If you teach your salespeople to maintain their focus, avoid distractions along the way, and concentrate the vast majority of their energies on this focus, they create amazing success stories. This presumes you focus also.

The late, great Earl Nightingale wrote about the "Law of Sacrificed Alternatives." Simply, anytime you choose to do something you automatically eliminate every other thing you could do *at that moment.* When you read one book, you eliminate all other books you could read at that moment; when you sit in a restaurant, you eliminate all other places you could be at that moment; and when you invest your sales time in one activity, you eliminate every other use of your time at that moment. With this principle, he articulated the urgency for people to invest their time prudently. The message for salespeople is clear: your focus and actions either move you closer to or farther away from your goals. As a manager, your challenge is to be a focusing expert to keep salespeople on course.

Activities

Scheduling determines how much time salespeople have for critical job functions. Statistics indicate that salespeople use less than one-third of their time in face-to-face selling activities. There are two implications you can draw from this. One, the time salespeople spend face-to-face needs to be quality time on quality prospects. Two, managers need to help salespeople better utilize their time so that there is more of it to spend with viable customers.

Prioritizing is a critical thinking skill essential to focusing. Most people set priorities according to whichever fire is burning the hottest. This is crisis management and largely reactive. A friend of mine joked one day about his firefighter's hat. He keeps it in his office because that's what he does all day: fights fires. How can you work on high priorities when you're constantly responding to everyone else's crises? Teach your salespeople to set priorities by payoff and importance.

High-payoff items are goal-oriented. Doing these moves you closer to where you want to be. It's the age-old time-management issue of efficiency and effectiveness. Efficiency is doing things right. Effectiveness is doing the right things. Naturally, you want both. Setting priorities is an effectiveness issue. You want your salespeople to work on the right things. What are the right things?

The Priority Matrix™ helps you instruct your staff how to focus with laser precision. Consider these two variables: payoff and urgency. Payoff refers to goal-directed. It moves the individual closer to achieving his goals—mission-directed. Urgency refers to time—how quickly something must be done. There are four possibilities: high-payoff/high-urgency, high-payoff/low-urgency, low-payoff/high-urgency, and low-payoff/low-urgency things. Refer to Figure 7 for a picture of this model.

FIGURE 7
PRIORITY MATRIX

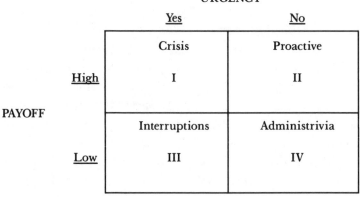

In quadrant I, you have high-payoff/high-urgency things to do. These are deadline-driven projects you must complete on time. It could include a call for immediate help from your largest customer. As you can see, payoff and time are major issues. Quadrant III is low payoff/high-urgency. This includes most telephone interruptions and miscellaneous requests from other people. You may notice a trend with urgent things. Many urgent items for you are *someone else's high-payoff things.* This is the dilemma most salespeople face. Do I work on my high-payoff things that propel me toward my goals or do I help other people complete their high-payoff items that help them achieve their goals?

Quadrant II, upper right-hand corner, includes high-payoff/low-urgency things that rarely get done but have great potential return on time invested. For example, goal setting, prospecting, training, getting a physical, writing a will, financial planning, etc. These never happen because of a lack of urgency. Quadrant IV activities include low-payoff/low-urgency things that don't really matter: administrivia.

If you pose the question of how to set priorities to your group, you hear: I, III, II, IV respectively. Two-thirds of the people I train set priorities by urgency not payoff. They spend most of their time extinguishing fires. At best, it's difficult to perform the type of value-added selling activities that support your goals when you're spending most of your time firefighting.

One way to help your salespeople live in quadrants I and II is to encourage them to stretch their time horizons: to think long-term. Long-term results come from high-payoff and not necessarily urgent activities. Your salespeople should ask themselves this question: "Does this activity lead me toward or away from my long-term goals?"

When you encourage your salespeople to plan by quadrant I and II activities, they move away from just being busy. The key to effective planning is to *schedule priorities not prioritize your schedule.* Begin the week by scheduling time for high-payoff activities (quadrants I and II). Once you have done that, allocate the rest of your time. You must do this every week.

Traditional planning is more activity-oriented, not priority-oriented. List everything that needs to be done and assign priorities. This encourages you to set priority by urgency.

One way to determine priorities is to examine critical job functions. What are the high-payoff job functions for your salespeople? Identify these and encourage your staff to build them into their week. This is focusing. Scheduling sales priorities means allocating time each week for prospecting, planning, self-development, and face-to-face offensive and defensive selling. Incorporate these priorities into a weekly checklist. On this checklist, include all high-payoff activities that create sales success. The list serves as a weekly reminder of what it takes to be goal-oriented.

Teaching your salespeople to think this way creates a pattern of sales effectiveness. They begin to live by solid time-management principles. They are acquiring one of the habits of success.

Accounts

Focusing applies to account selection, too. Critical to the success of value-added sales management is your focusing the salesforce on high-priority accounts that produce the return you want. In Chapter 2, I called these Jumbo CDs and offered tips for selecting them. Companies have various systems for account classification. These methods usually include volume, potential, and hopefully profit.

Some organizations use the Paretto Principle: the 80/20 rule. The top 20 percent of your accounts yield 80 percent of your volume. These are A accounts. Bs and Cs are then classified separately. Other companies use the one-third method. As, Bs, and Cs each count as one-third.

A variation of the 80/20 rule is the 15-20-65 method. The top 15 percent of your accounts produce 65 percent of your revenue, the next 20 percent produce 20 percent of your sales, and the bottom 65 percent produce only 15 percent of your revenue. Respectively, these are A, B, and C accounts.

With the 15-20-65 method, allocating sales time is remarkably simple. Use this formula: $A = 2B = 4C$. Call on A accounts twice as often as B accounts and four times as often as C accounts. This gives maximum coverage in all three segments.

The advantage of this or any method is that you *systematically* allocate your time in the field. Strategically focusing your salespeople gives you a substantial competitive advantage because fewer than 5 percent of all salespeople do it.

Pipelines

Keeping salespeople focused also means creating a steady flow of business opportunities, aka the sales pipeline. Conceive of a model that incorporates immediate business, intermediate business, and long-term business opportunities: Red-Hot Prospects (RHP), Viable Candidates (VC), and Prospects (P) respectively.

RHPs are pieces of business that will *probably* happen in the short-term—"when" versus "if" business. You're very sure that these will happen. Your salespeople spend a great deal of time with these accounts working out details, hand holding, and working on the final commitment. It's almost money in the bank.

VCs are pieces of business that will *possibly* happen: more intermediate than short-term—"if" versus "when." Your salespeople spend a lot of time developing this business. There are no guarantees here; and in many cases, your salespeople allow themselves to become "prisoners of hope" to these buyers.

Ps are pieces of business where you sense an opportunity. There is fire somewhere inside that smoke. Pursuing this business is filling the pipeline. They are the "maybes" and the "desirables." You would love to have this business, feel that you have a reasonable chance for getting it, and don't mind the time investment it takes to pursue it.

Every salesperson has a pipeline—full or not. Based on national closing ratios, focus your staff this way: for every one RHP, they need two VCs and four Ps. This keeps a steady flow of business opportunities and prevents your salespeople from working on too many VCs that promise a lot but deliver nothing. Generally, the VC level is where most salespeople delude themselves into believing that one more call will make the difference. A fistful of bonafide Ps make letting go of VCs easy. A consistent prospecting effort keeps the pipeline full and your salespeople focused on success.

FEEDBACK

Imagine walking into a performance-appraisal session with your boss, and he begins to unload on you with things you never heard before. He's accumulated lists of rules infractions, mistakes, and wrong decisions you've made over the past year. This is your annual stoning. Imagine another scenario—never getting feedback from your boss. He keeps you guessing. You never know how you're doing because he doesn't tell you. Extreme? Yes! Uncommon? No!

I wonder how many salespeople operate in a fog about the quality of their performance. Many know about quantitative things like percent of quota. But how many think about the *quality* of their efforts? That's the essence of feedback. Sales managers have some unique opportunities to provide this type of feedback: before calls, after joint calls, in monthly sales reports, during special coaching and counseling sessions, etc.

Joint Calling

Joint calling is mandatory for performance feedback. Without it, you can only deliver quantitative feedback to salespeople. You can only "guesstimate" the quality of their efforts. How often to joint call is a judgment that only you can determine. Some salespeople require more attention than others.

During the precall phase, ask the salesperson these three questions:

1. What do you want to accomplish on this call?
2. What *action* do you want from the customer at the end of the call?
3. How will you reinforce value-added on the call?

These questions help focus salespeople. It gives you a framework for providing feedback after each call. You can measure whether or not salespeople achieve these objectives during the call.

Formalizing the joint call process alerts salespeople that you take this seriously. Using standard feedback forms, having routine times established for joint calling, and having a policy that supports these efforts sends a strong message to the salesforce. They say you're serious about this process. Formalizing also means joint calling as a policy, not a punishment for missing quota. Sell it as a benefit to the salesperson—an in-the-field training program. Point out that everyone joint calls. It's part of the company's success formula.

When discussing performance, sandwich your feedback. Begin with something positive about the call, offer specific behavioral feedback with corrective action, and follow up with another positive statement about the call. Use this pattern: compliment, constructive behavioral criticism with corrective action, compliment. You may have to look long and hard to find something positive to reinforce, but it's worth the effort.

Focus on tangibles—behaviors. Steer clear of vague issues like attitude even though there's a great tendency for managers to discuss "bad attitudes." If you sense that attitude is an issue, behavioralize it. Present it as something measurable like increased cynical comments, excessive complaining, never offering positive input, etc.

While on the call, remain silent and let the salesperson do the talking. You're there to observe not sell. Watch for listening skills and nonverbal communication. Analyze the dynamics of the relationship between the customer and your salesperson. Your folks are going to be nervous so be empathic. Focus on significant issues. Don't nitpick.

Debrief after each call. Your feedback has less impact at the end of the day. Review the call step-by-step and refer to the call-objective questions from the precall phase. Give feedback to your reps on their achieving those objectives. Use the following checklist to focus on specific selling tasks.

- Did the rep have clear precall objectives?
- Did the rep state these objectives early in the opening stage?
- Did the rep establish rapport with the buyer?
- Were the questions open-ended?
- Did the questions follow the needs-analysis format?
- Was the presentation customized to the buyer's needs?
- Did the rep ask for something from the buyer? (close the sale)

- How effectively did the rep answer the customer's objections?
- How will the rep follow up from here?

When coaching and counseling, focus on the *behavior you want* not the behavior you don't want. For example, concentrate on the new business you want your salespeople to pursue, not the fact that they haven't cold called in years. Positive wording creates a positive focus. You might say, "I want you to sell more profitably," instead of "Quit discounting."

If and when employees become defensive, ensure that you're trying to fix the problem and not the blame. There's a difference between excuses and explanations. When employees get defensive, they try to excuse behavior with explanations.

Counseling Model

This model helps you professionalize your coaching and counseling sessions. It ensures that you assertively and empathically communicate with your employee.

Preparation. Give some thought in advance to what you want to say, how you can best say it, and what you want this meeting to produce.

Opening phase. State the purpose of the meeting, make a statement about the problem, and tell why it's a problem. For example:

> Frank, I wanted to meet with you today to discuss a concern I have regarding your cold calling efforts. As you know, we've implemented a cold calling campaign to increase new business. Most of the salesforce has bought into this concept and we're beginning to see some very positive results. The problem is that you haven't been cold calling and I feel that you're missing opportunities in your territory for new business.

Exchange phase. Get the employee's input or understanding of the situation, agree on goals and strategies (expose any barriers), and ask for a commitment to action.

Follow-up phase. Check back with the employee, monitor the employee's performance, and make the appropriate changes.

A real benefit of this model is the controlled atmosphere for discussing some potentially explosive issues. You're treating the employee with respect and dignity while asserting your point of view. You get the results you need and he gets constructive feedback on improved performance.

COMPENSATION

Money is not the universal motivator. On the other hand, for salespeople it is one indicator of their performance and an incentive to sell more. For the past eleven years, I've worked with hundreds of companies and I can't remember two compensation programs that were exactly the same. Some pay commissions on gross sales—others pay on gross margins. Some pay no incentive—others pay only commission. Some pay salespeople their incentive monthly—others pay quarterly. The only rule seems to be that there are no rules.

Like so many topics in this chapter, compensation has its own experts and books on the topic. I address it in this chapter because it is a critical dynamic in a sales management system. Also, the spin I put on compensation should reflect the overall topic of this book, value-added selling.

Recent statistics offer some ideas on how companies compensate salespeople:

- 28% salary only
- 12% commission only
- 53% salary and commission
- 8% salary and bonus

Notice that this does not add up to 100 percent. I rounded the fractions off—much to the chagrin of the detail types reading this. I find it interesting that three out of every four salespeople are paid a dollar incentive to increase business. This is self-employment! It supports the position that salespeople really are in business for themselves with someone else's money.

The most creative and positive compensation program I've ever seen is the Target Income Plan (TIP). At the beginning of the year, the sales manager and salesperson establish sales quotas and objectives. The compensation package is 50 percent salary and 50 percent commission; hence, the target income. The salesperson receives the target income if she achieves 100 percent of her quota. The target income is twice her salary. The advantage is that management and the salesperson speak in terms of target income. It's a conversation of what she's targeted to earn this year. A forty-thousand-dollar-a-year salesperson is now an eighty-thousand-dollar-a-year salesperson *in her mind*. Spending habits expand with this reworked self-image and the sales behavior follows. She feels like an eighty-thousand-dollar-a-year earner.

TIP spotlights the goal, reinforces and expands the self-image, and provides the incentive to achieve it. It addresses the emotional as well as the financial aspects of compensation. This list of questions helps you examine your compensation program to ensure that it does what you want it to do:

- What do we want to reward?
- Do we want to reinforce cold or repeat calling?
- Which product lines do we want to reward?
- Do we want to reinforce volume or profit sales?
- Will we reward for creative sales ideas?
- Do we reward self-development?
- Other than money, what else can we use?

- Does our compensation package encourage a career in sales?
- Do we compensate unlimited performance or cap earnings?
- Can our salespeople earn more than management?
- Are we giving as good as we're getting?
- Is team or individual compensation preferred in our case?
- Should we reward for offensive or defensive selling efforts?
- Can we reward salespeople for customer satisfaction?
- Should we compensate the team involved in the sale?

There are many variables that influence your decision to compensate salespeople. Add to this discussion the topic of independent reps and you have an entirely different scenario. Basically, you must design a program that supports your company goals. Challenge yourself on the issue of rewarding gross sales or gross margin. This is a book on value-added selling. And since value-added is a philosophy of maximum performance and not minimum standards, why would you limit or cap your salespeople's performance earnings? It's a mixed message to your salesforce. Pay on profit for unlimited performance.

CHAPTER SUMMARY

This chapter started out to be the same length as the other chapters in this book. It ended up being the longest. I didn't just get long-winded when I wrote it. The underlying message is that these key sales management dynamics are critical to your success. At the very minimum, these elements must be in place for a strong sales management system. It's your checklist. By studying these ideas, you are able to explore each topic individually with more depth as needed. This is only the starting point.

7
Motivation

The most persistent question sales managers ask me is, "How do I motivate my salespeople?" It's a topic that fascinates educators and frustrates parents, bosses, and coaches.

Understanding motivation provides you with insight into your own motivated behavior and knowledge about what impels your salespeople to act in a certain way. Applying its principles enables you to create an environment that is highly motivating for the individual. You can predict and create behavior that is mutually rewarding.

In this chapter, I introduce a performance formula that explains why some achieve and others do not, principles of motivation, a motivation matrix that gives you insight into behavior, and prescriptions for creating highly motivating work environments.

WHAT IS PERFORMANCE?

The most intellectually stimulating day in my educational career came one evening as I sat in a graduate psychology course. The professor wrote a formula on the board and explained it to the group.

$$P = M \times A$$

Performance is a function of your motivation times your ability. It's a mathematical relationship in which one variable compensates for the other. For example, do you know someone who is a ten (on a ten-point scale) when it comes to ability and a two when it comes to motivation? This performance score is a twenty. This person has all the ability in the world but for some reason can't muster the drive to do anything with it.

On the other hand, do you know anyone with average ability (say, a five) but a ten on motivation? That person scores a fifty on performance and beats the other one hands down every time. And he does it with pure motivation—guts, drive, persistence, or whatever you want to call it.

The more I considered that formula the more excited I got. It means you can take an average performer and turn her into a superstar by working on motivation. Our culture is filled with a lot of ordinary people doing extraordinary things. Something that's even more exciting is that the ability factor in this equation has two elements: innate and acquired ability.

Innate ability is the stuff you're born with—your genetic predisposition. Acquired ability is what you learn along the way. What you're reading today enhances your acquired ability. The implication is that you can help your salespeople become superstars because of what you teach them and the motivational climate you create.

As a sales manager, you live by these two questions:

1. What am I teaching my salespeople today to help them achieve their potential?
2. How am I creating a motivational climate for my salespeople?

Asking and answering these questions guides your motivational program. Much of what I covered in the last chapter focused on the dynamics of a leadership system.

This chapter focuses more on how managers guide and inspire their people.

WHAT IS MOTIVATION?

Motivation is the energy *within* the individual that excites, incites, and ignites behavior. Noticed the italicized word *within*. This is critical to understanding motivation. It happens inside the person. Stimulation, on the other hand, happens outside the individual. The distinction is more than semantics. It's how you effect behavior in others. You may *stimulate* a response but something inside the person *motivates* the behavior. This distinction becomes clearer as we move forward with the discussion.

Rules of Motivation

You can't motivate another person. This naturally follows the previous paragraph. Since motivation is an internal process, the best you can hope to accomplish is to create an environment in which the other person's internal motivation takes over to impel the behavior you desire. Please reread that last sentence. *It's inside the other person.* Your job is to arouse it, stimulate it, activate it, and give it an opportunity for expression. The needs and the energy are in place. How you tap into them determines the response you get.

The classic example of leading a horse to water and not being able to make it drink illustrates this concept. The horse can be influenced to drink if you run it hard or salt its food, but the desire or need to drink comes from within the horse. You merely stimulated it. You gave it the opportunity for expression.

Everyone is motivated. Imagine the arguments I hear from sales managers in my seminars over this idea. Because motivation is used erroneously, people automatically assume that because someone fails to perform in a way that the observer values, the other person is "unmotivated." I submit that the other person *is* motivated *not* to perform in that fashion.

The blue-collar worker has taken an unfair rap for years for being "unmotivated." I suggest that you visit a plant around closing time and stand in front of the time clock. You'll get stampeded in the rush to leave. That's a motivated work force. They're motivated to get out of there! Perhaps they would be less motivated to leave if management did something to make it a more challenging and exciting environment in which to work. This example brings up our next important key to understanding motivation.

People do things for their reasons. Not yours. In fact, they probably don't even care what your reasons are. Buyers buy for their reasons not yours. Salespeople work for their reasons not yours. One man's pleasure is another man's poison. Values play a big role in assessing motivated behavior. If an employee does something that a manager values, the manager perceives the employee as motivated. If the employee engages in some other non–goal-directed behavior, the manager perceives him as unmotivated.

Sales managers get into trouble with motivation when they allow their personal values to affect their perception of an employee's motivation. For example, I've had a number of managers scratch their heads wanting to know why an unlimited commission program does not "motivate" their salespeople for that last big push at the end of the year. Maybe the salesperson does not *value* money the same way the manager does. Remember the three-hundred-dollar briefcase for the telemarketers? The boss couldn't understand why the employees didn't *value* it the way he did. He was jamming a hollow compensation program down their throats and couldn't figure out why they were acting like ingrates.

Let's go back to the beginning of the book. Value, like beauty, is in the eye of the beholder. Beware of allowing your values to bias your perception. People are motivated. They are motivated to pursue what's important to them. The relevant question is, "Are you motivated to give it to them?" No more than you would support a product-driven approach to sales, why would you support a management-driven versus an employee-driven approach to motivation?

Principles of Motivation

The following list of ideas is a primer on motivated behavior and how you can encourage its expression. Use these fundamental principles to guide your management approach.

People rise (and fall) to their levels of expectations. As early as the 1960s, researchers were discovering that a manager's expectations for a subordinate's performance influence the way the manager treats the employee. The manager's behavior in turn creates an environment for high or low achievement. Managers who believe their employees are capable of achieving great things act in ways to support this belief and fashion working environments that encourage high achievement. On the other hand, when managers expect little, that's what they receive. They communicate that message, too.

From my personal experiences as a manager, I've discovered that I pretty much get back what I *expect* to see in my employees. It's as if I'm looking for the behavior and either consciously or unconsciously reinforce it. What's unconscious for me is highly visible for my employees.

The eighteenth-century German poet Goethe wrote, "Treat people as if they were what they ought to be and you help them become what they are capable of becoming." He didn't need hard-core scientific research to figure out that we either help or hurt people by our expectations and behavior.

Everyone has different levels of needs with varying capacities for satisfaction. Motivation is such a uniquely personal thing that each of us has a motivational profile as individual as our fingerprints. Some people have an insatiable desire for praise, recognition, and affiliation while others prefer autonomy and anonymity. Why do some people crave strawberry ice cream and others could go the rest of their lives without ever eating it? To understand motivation, you must realize that each salesperson who works for you is motivated by a uniquely different set of needs than everyone else on the staff. Your understanding of these fine distinctions enables you to respond with a management approach that inspires action by your staff.

What works for one may not necessarily work for another. There is no universal motivator. You must experiment like a scientist to design the right formula for each person. Having done that, you've reduced much of the guesswork in management.

Environments that offer challenge, demand creativity, and encourage growth are highly motivating. These work environments tap into the employee's higher-level needs. By encouraging employees to meet these needs and giving them the opportunity, you create a work force that is motivated to meet these needs on the job. Employees meet these needs either on or off the job. Why not give them a chance to be excited about their work?

Involvement and participation lower resistance to change. Management studies continue to show that involving employees in the change process lowers their resistance and builds commitment to the change. As you implement a value-added selling program in your organization, it's imperative to involve your people from the start to build commitment.

Intimidation is a short-term motivator. Intimidation
works, but only short-term. People recoil at the constant
barrage of criticism and threats that accompany intimidation. Sales managers who hold threat sessions instead of
inspirational and instructional meetings soon learn that
the salesforce would rather have a root canal than attend
one of their sessions. There's grave insecurity in a manager
who only uses coercion to move others.

Six Prescriptions for Managers

People are motivated if these things happen. Guide your
approach to reflect these prescriptions.

  • *They feel they can achieve the desired behavior.* "If I
try, can I make it happen?" When people individually ask
themselves this question, they need a positive response. If
the answer is no, focus on the reasons. They must perceive
few obstacles. Barrier analysis prevents barrier paralysis.

  • *They feel challenged, not defeated.* Too much challenge, like too little challenge, is demotivating. People
want to feel that they have a reasonable chance of achieving their goals. How motivating is it to pursue the impos-
sible dream?

  • *Their behavior has a desired payoff.* Employees naturally ask this question: "What's in it for me?" If it's positive for them, they will move heaven and earth to get it. If
it lacks personal value, apathy results.

  • *They perceive that management treats them equitably.* By and large, everyone wants to feel that she is getting
as good as she is giving. Employees need to feel that this
"boomerang effect" applies to their efforts and rewards.
This is one reason why salespeople are paid differently
from other employees. The direct impact of their efforts as
producers is highly visible to management and the salesforce. Imagine someone creating several million dollars
worth of business and not sharing in the profits?

- *They have an internalized sense of mission.* When employees buy into the mission, their commitment factor is higher. They feel like they're part of something bigger than themselves. They learn that "we" is a lot stronger than "me."

- *They feel a sense of meaningfulness to what they do.* Imagine how boring it would be to work in a job that you felt was menial and meaningless—that if you didn't do it, it wouldn't matter anyway. Everyone needs to feel that he is relevant and contributes in some fashion. I know one sales manager who constantly reminds his salespeople of the number of other employees and their families who depend on the salesforce to keep the company going. It's his way to make the staff realize the importance of sales.

This section provided you with information on the conditions under which people are motivated to perform on the job. The most fundamental principle in motivation is that it exists within the individual. Managers who understand and accept this find it easier to tap into this achievement energy.

MOTIVATION THEORIES

In management psychology, there are three schools of thought on motivation theory. Each has its own merits. Each works. When I present each of these in management seminars, some people prefer one over the others because it suits their individual styles. As you read through this section, select the one that fits you best and use it for your staff. In reading the others you may notice some similarities beneath the surface.

Content Models

Content theorists believe in the "what" of motivation . . . *what* motivates the person. They explain motivated behavior in terms of what force moves the person. Typically, this force is an unmet need. Need impels action. This is a need-satisfaction model of behavior. Accordingly, everyone has needs that must be met and behavior is the expression of this need satisfaction.

Three popular content theorists are Maslow, Herzberg, and Alderfer. Their theories vary in labeling needs, but for the most part, they agree on an ascending order of sophistication for these needs. Simply, we all have different levels of needs. The Motivation Matrix™ diagram (Figure 8) summarizes their philosophies in an applications-oriented model.

Notice that there are three levels of needs: basic, social, and growth. Other labels also work: basic, midlevel, and

FIGURE 8
MOTIVATION MATRIX™

		PERSONAL	BUSINESS	MOTIVATORS
ASCENDING ORDER	GROWTH	• Actualization • Achievement • Esteem • Independence	• Advancement • Challenging work • Titles	• Opportunities to advance • Opportunities to learn • Job enrichment • Increased control • Participation
	SOCIAL	• Status • Love • Belongingness	• Acceptance • Professional relationships • Respect of peers	• Praise and recognition • Socialization • Compliments • Group activities
	BASIC	• Safety • Stability • Food, air, sex, etc.	• Working conditions • Benefits • Money	• Status quo • Incentives • Money, bonuses, etc. • Favorable working conditions

higher-order needs. The labels are less important than the concepts. These key points will help you understand the content theories:

• *Each of us has different levels of needs, arranged hierarchically in an ascending order of sophistication—basic to complex.* The basic-level needs are those for food, air, water, sex, shelter, etc. Midlevel needs focus on the sense of belongingness that everyone must feel. Higher-level needs include the needs for independence, autonomy, creative expression, and self-actualization.

• *For whatever reasons, each of us has varying requirements for need-satisfaction at each level.* This explains why some people focus more on satisfying one level of need over another. As a content theorist, you're not concerned with why someone fixates on one level of needs over another. You simply accept that to some people meeting one level of needs is more important than meeting another. It would be interesting to conjecture an opinion on why one is more important, but it's irrelevant for this model.

• *Once a level of need has been satisfied, it no longer has the same motivational impact on behavior.* This explains why money ceases to be a powerful motivator when the salesperson's financial needs are met. Time and again I hear from sales managers, "I can't understand why my salespeople aren't motivated by our compensation program." It's because their money needs are being met.

• *Once a need is satisfied, we are drawn to the next-higher level of need.* For example, when your basic-level needs are satisfied, you are drawn to meet the next-higher level of needs, and this continues until you reach a peak experience called self-actualization. Maslow defined self-actualization as "becoming more and more of what you're capable of becoming" and said it's like a drug: the more you experience it, the more you want it.

In the Motivation Matrix, I've listed personal needs in the left-hand column, concomitant business needs in the center column, and business motivators in the right-hand column. A benefit of this model is that you're able to parallel basic-level business needs with basic-level personal needs.

Drawing from the content theorists' models, once an employee's basic-level needs for salary, benefits, decent working conditions, and stability are met, the employee is motivated to satisfy higher-level needs such as professional acceptance, respect of peers, opportunities for advancement, creative expression, and self-actualization. They're ascending the hierarchy. The good news is that you have the potential for helping employees meet these needs on the job.

There are a number of implications for this model. Let's pick up on our last point.

• *These needs will be met.* People find ways to meet these needs on or off the job. People who work in mundane, confining, and restrictive jobs find ways off the job to meet their upper-level needs. They go home and carve ducks, compose music, tie fishing lures, join social clubs, write poetry, become active in church leadership roles, and so on. These are positive expressions. It's a shame that management doesn't recognize and unleash this talent on the job.

• *Enrich the job.* Herzberg prescribed job enrichment as a way for managers to create a more highly motivating environment for workers. This encourages managers to focus on helping the employees meet higher-level needs on the job. His position was simple. You can have workers who are not really dissatisfied with their working conditions but who are not particularly motivated by the demands of the job. These folks will go through the motions. His remedy is to make the jobs more meaningful, empower the employees, and provide opportunities for challenge and creativity.

• *Balance your approach.* The most creative application of this model comes from a sales manager who used this model to redesign his management approach and the sales job in his company. He realized that no two salespeople have the same motivational profile. He accepted that everyone "lives" on one level of need satisfaction more than another. Consequently, he began to notice which level of needs were more important to different employees and then tried to find a way to help them satisfy those needs. Second, he redesigned the job so that every salesperson had an opportunity to meet all levels of needs on the job. He compensated them, built stability into the job, encouraged peer relationships, gave them recognition opportunities, and opened the job for their continuous professional development. They grew with the jobs, forged strong peer relationships that nurtured teamwork, and the company reaped the benefits.

Your shaping the work environment to meet all levels of needs is a positive first step in the right direction. Your accepting that everyone has a unique profile of needs sensitizes you to the individuality of your salespeople. I believe that the levels of needs are far more interactive and dynamic than they appear on the surface. It's conceivable that an employee can achieve self-actualization and still focus on meeting other levels of needs.

I'm passionate on growth needs. "Actualist psychologists" believe that humans are born as goal-driven organisms that strive to become "more and more" each day. How many people wake up in the morning, look in the mirror, and say, "Yeah. Today I'm going out there and be mediocre. When it comes to being average, I'm the best"? It doesn't happen. People want to be better today than they were yesterday, and better tomorrow than today. Your job as a sales manager is to help your salespeople achieve that goal.

Offering your salespeople a compensation package that satisfies their lower-level needs, recognizing and celebrating their achievements, and giving them opportunities to grow intellectually creates an environment of mutual respect and commitment. Not a bad place to start.

Process Models

Process models of motivation focus on the choices people make in selecting behavior. Perception and cognition are important to these models. To process theorists, motivation is goal-directed behavior resulting from choices individuals make after evaluating perceived outcomes. Whereas the content models focus on the "what" of behavior, the process models concentrate on the "why" of behavior. Expectancy theory is at the forefront of the process models.

The premise of expectancy theory is that individuals evaluate various behavioral strategies and then select the ones they perceive as most likely to bring about the rewards they desire. There are three important variables in this process:

1. *Expectancy perceptions*—these refer to the person's beliefs about their ability to engage successfully in certain goal-directed behavior. "If I attempt to cold call, can I be successful?"
2. *Instrumentality perceptions*—this refers to the likelihood of receiving the desired reward if the person engages in the behavior. "If I do cold call, is there something in it for me?"
3. *Valence perceptions*—this refers to the relative desirability of the reward. "Is the payoff worth it?"

Behavior results from perceptions and choices surrounding these three conditions: the person feels capable of achieving a certain behavior, believes that the behavior leads to rewards, and the rewards are valuable to the person.

The manager's role in this is to help the employee with his perceptions and choices. Begin with the expectancy perceptions. Can the salesperson be successful if he tries? Perhaps a more appropriate question is, "What barriers impede the salesperson from successfully performing a certain behavior?" Real or perceived doesn't matter. They're all real to the salesperson. In my work, I find that this first question offers great potential for making a difference in motivation.

Let's examine a scenario. What barriers inhibit your staff from selling value-added? Could it be product issues, company issues, literature issues, customer priorities, competitive pressures, market conditions, or lack of skills and training? Any of these de-motivate . . . collectively, they're demoralizing. These barriers answer the expectancy perception question.

Couple this scenario with no reward for value-added selling (instrumentality perceptions) or one that means little to the salesperson (valence perceptions) and you have a formula for disaster.

Living and managing by these three questions makes life easier and more productive for everyone. Climb inside the salesperson's skin and ask yourself these three questions from his perspective:

1. If I try, can I be successful?
2. If I am successful, is there a payoff?
3. Is the payoff worth it to me?

In my opinion, the last question links the content and process models. The reward has greater value when it meets some need of the individual.

Reinforcement Models

The reinforcement model is the behaviorist's philosophy. Behavior is maintained by its consequences. Shape the behavior you want, reinforce it, and the person will repeat it. Many people dislike this model because it smacks of lab rats and conditioning. Whether you like it or not doesn't matter. Your behavior and your subordinates' is reinforced constantly with rewards or punishment. Others shape your behavior as much as you shape other people's behavior. No one lives in a vacuum or is insulated from others reinforcing his behavior.

Behaviorism's appeal is its simple linkage between behavior and response. Since it deals with behavior, not cognition, it's easily measurable. Managers like that also. Behaviorism offers easy-to-understand principles:

- There must be a link between behavior and reinforcement.
- The shorter the interval between behavior and reinforcement, the more powerful the reward.
- The value of the reinforcement (valence) to the individual affects subsequent behavior.

Managers shape desired responses by rewarding movement toward the behavior. They begin by telling the employee what behavior is expected and then reinforce successive approximations (baby steps) toward it. Smart managers reinforce the effort initially. For some people, trying is good enough. Putting forth effort is a positive first step in behavioral change. Expecting too much too soon creates goal anxiety and inhibits performance instead of encouraging it. As the effort becomes permanent behavior, shift your focus to qualitative and quantitative measurements: quality of effort and results.

For example, if you have a salesperson who hates to cold call and hasn't done much of it lately, try this approach. First, state the expectation. Tell him he must cold call. Give him a target number. Explain that you're more interested in his efforts and experiences at this point. Inform him that you want to meet to discuss the calls at the end of the day (short interval). In your review, praise the effort, reward him for trying, and acknowledge that you know how difficult it is for him to make these calls.

Repeat this process for a permanent behavioral change. Gradually shift your focus to results. While doing this, avoid numbers anxiety. Focus initially on the quality of the efforts while building awareness for viability of the efforts. Give performance feedback on application of skills, e.g., "How many times did you ask for the order?" The relationship between effort and reward must remain strong. Clarifying activity goals and shifting the focus eventually minimizes early feelings of defeat.

These tips will help you with your reinforcement schedules:

- The quickest way to shape behavior is to reinforce it every time the person demonstrates it.
- The quickest way to extinguish behavior is to stop reinforcing it.
- Once a desired level of behavior is achieved, intermittently reinforce it to sustain repetition. This is especially true if you use the on-the-average principle. On the average, reward the behavior every fifth performance. You're like a slot machine. You do not pay out every fifth time, you pay out every fifth time *on the average.*
- Praise is the most inexpensive and highly visible reinforcer you can use. Recognizing performance in front of others exponentially increases its worth. The opposite is true for reprimanding. Do it in private. Respect for the individual pays off in the long run.
- Developing a reinforcement program for your salespeople involves these questions: What behavior do I want? What reinforcers do they value? How will I help them acquire the behavior? How will I reinforce their sustaining the behavior?

The principles of behaviorism do not mean dark psychology labs with animals being shocked into submission. It can be a very positive experience for the manager and the subordinate. You've been doing and receiving it all of your life. Becoming more aware of how to implement it can enhance your motivational efforts.

THE MOTIVATIONAL PLAN

Taking the best from all three models and developing a motivational plan for your salesforce is a great challenge. These ideas will help.

- Offer opportunities for all levels of needs to be met on the job.
- Identify at which level of needs the salesperson mostly operates.
- Build personal and professional growth into the job.
- Enrich the job. Ask salespeople for their input on how to do this.
- Identify and eliminate internal and external barriers that interfere with your salespeople performing their job the way they want to.
- Is there a payoff for the salesperson's behavior?
- Is the payoff worth it?
- Does the salesperson perceive equity between his input on the job and what he gets out of the job? Is he getting as good as he's giving?
- What behavior do you want from the salesperson?
- How will you reinforce it?
- Are you focusing on results or effort?

CHAPTER SUMMARY

In this chapter, I've emphasized that motivation is a personal issue. Everyone's motivational profile is as unique as her fingerprints. Approach each person individually. Since motivation is an internal concept, the best you can hope to accomplish is to create an environment that stimulates the person's internal motivation to want to successfully engage in desired behaviors. Reinforcing these behaviors ensures the likelihood that they will recur.

Management is an active, not static, process. Developing a management plan and executing, testing, and modifying it are part of the process.

8
The Plateaued Salesperson

"Did you ever think you were in a groove but discovered you're in a rut?" When I ask this question in seminars, salespeople grin with guilt. They find it amusing and revealing. An experienced salesman came up to me one day and said, "Tom, you know the only difference between a rut and a grave is the size of the hole you're in!" We laughed about it for a few moments. How true it is.

Current studies prove that one out of every four salespeople is in a comfort zone. Further, 97 percent of those companies surveyed report they are having trouble with plateaued salespeople. For salespeople, it's a "when" issue—not an "if" issue.

In this chapter, I focus on this interesting phenomenon. I explore the reasons and the remedies: why people hit plateaus, why they choose to stay there, and how they can blast off of them.

WHAT IS A COMFORT ZONE?

A comfort zone is what you're accustomed to—your mental neighborhood. It's where you grew up, your father's job, your mother's education level, where you went to school, your birth order, who your friends were, how well you performed in sports, how much support you got along the way, your religious background, your job training, your first sales manager, your spouse's background, the last neighborhood you lived in: the sum total and synergy of your collective life experiences. Comfort zones apply to all areas in our lives—business and personal.

The word *comfort* is a misnomer because it could be a discomfort zone: something you dislike but are used to. You may not be comfortable with something, just familiar with it. You don't really have to be comfortable to be in a comfort zone. All you have to be is stuck in a mode that you're accustomed to—good or bad.

For example, buyers continue to purchase from suppliers that ship late because they're used to it. Buyers adjust lead times to reflect it. Some people stay in a bad relationship because it's familiar, and they feel stuck. To some, familiar pain beats the unknown. Therefore, they stay with what they know. They may even adopt coping strategies for the familiar pain to cushion its impact.

A performance plateau is a behavioral response to an emotional decision to remain in a comfort zone. A plateau is a flat area where you stop doing whatever got you to where you are. It's going through the motions, showing up, doing just enough to get by. Some call it the spectator syndrome. For salespeople, this means failing to develop new business, selling tried and true product lines versus new product groups, and calling on the same customers without expanding your base.

Are comfort zones good or bad? It depends whom you ask. Managers respond with the perfunctory, "There's no room in our company for plateaued salespeople." The successful salesperson may respond, "I've earned the right to kick back a little and enjoy my success." It seems reasonable to me that there are times in our lives when people need a breather, time to regroup and recharge. These are rest areas not parking zones.

A more relevant question than "good or bad" is, "Is it phasal or final?" If it's phasal, maybe the salesperson is regrouping for another surge in performance—a recess instead of a retreat. If it's final, then it sounds a lot like death—i.e., mentally expiring.

A danger of being in a comfort zone is the reactive nature of plateauing. Customers perceive it and don't like it. The "wait-and-see" attitude misses a lot of opportunities. In a competitive business environment there is very little room for long-term resting on one's laurels. Prolonged plateauing may even lead to a lifestyle change. Passivity in one area may spill over into other areas. For salespeople, the real danger is the risk of going from a profit center to a cost center. There's no future in becoming an expense item.

ARE YOU IN A COMFORT ZONE?

So how do you know if you or your salespeople are in a comfort zone? Usually when you're in one you know it (at some gut level) and get defensive over the issue. The intensity of the denial may be your primary indicator. In terms of attitude, you notice an increase in cynical remarks and waning enthusiasm. You send behavioral signals: going through the motions, doing just enough to get by, and procrastinating.

The following quiz provides an objective indicator. Answer yes or no to each item; give yourself one point for each "yes" answer.

- You can't remember the name of the last book you read on your profession.
- Your work needs to be corrected and redone.
- You show a lack of follow-through.

- You work fewer hours than you used to.
- You resist management systems and paperwork.
- You live in the past.
- You're late with paperwork.
- You show increased absenteeism.
- Everything feels repetitive and too predictable.
- You have a feeling of being too weighed down by responsibilities (trapped).
- You've shifted to a more passive attitude.
- You have low initiative and enthusiasm.
- You're indecisive and withdrawn.
- You procrastinate.
- You're failing to generate new ideas.
- You demonstrate self-sabotaging behavior.
- You're failing to establish and pursue goals.
- You're doing only what's required.
- You're making more cynical comments.
- You resent everything because it impinges on your time.
- You have a feeling of coasting.
- You've been downgrading your objectives.

A score of 0–2 "yes" answers puts you with the top 18 percent of those taking this test—whom I call "extra milers." A 3–6 score puts you with the 57 percent who are borderline "comfortable." And 7 or more earns you a place with the 25 percent who are definitely in a comfort zone (maybe even a parking zone!).

WHY PEOPLE STAY IN COMFORT ZONES

One reason people stay in comfort zones is that they are inhibited by some external constraint. Confining job descriptions, economic limitations, and other external reasons may discourage people from blasting out of a comfort zone. More commonly, things inside the person inhibit their stretching out of comfort zones.

In the comfort-zone model (Figure 9), notice the concentric rings with shaded areas between them. The innermost ring is your comfort zone. The outer rings are progressive levels of potential. The shaded areas represent your "Anxiety Zones." Each time you stretch beyond one ring to the next you feel change anxiety. It's a natural part of the change dynamic. The critical factor is what you *do* with that anxiety. Some allow it to overwhelm them, and it pulls them back like a gravitational force into their comfort zones. For others, it's an adrenaline rush: the surge of energy to reach the next level of performance.

For some, the pull of this change anxiety is overpowering. These folks resist change—the fear of the unknown, the untried, or the unproven. Change is a scary concept for many people. Because of it they remain with what's familiar even if it's uncomfortable. One study indicates that 70

FIGURE 9

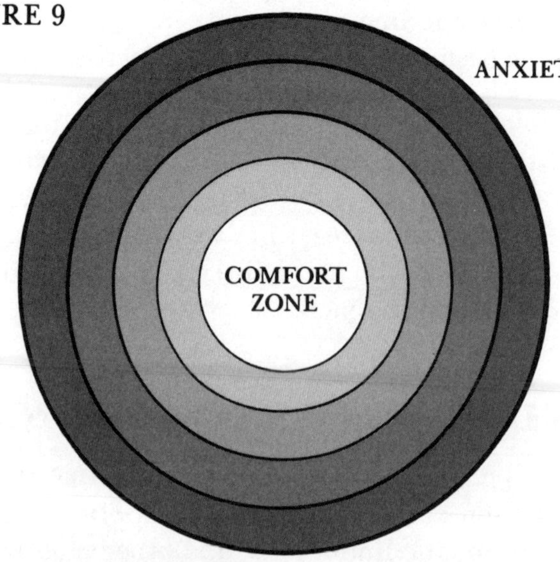

ANXIETY ZONES

COMFORT ZONE

AREA OF POTENTIAL

percent of the people in the United States are low-risk individuals. For them, change is more anxiety-provoking than exciting.

Others view change as an admission that they are "insufficient" the way they are. They confuse growth and stretching to one's potential with not being "good enough" as is. They become defensive when presented with growth suggestions.

A third reason why salespeople stay in comfort zones is laziness. I believe that this is the least common of the six reasons. I'm too optimistic to believe that a substantial percentage of the population is lazy. Low self-esteem? Maybe. Low self-confidence? Probably. Lazy? No.

A fourth reason is being comfortable. There are people who truly are comfortable with the life they have created. More power to them. They have reached a point that most aspire to: comfortable and contributing. I believe these people are a minority. Comfortable and complacent is different than comfortable and contributing.

A fifth and common reason is the fear of failure. Failing to achieve one's goals can be expensive financially and emotionally. For those whose self-esteem is tied to their performance, failure is devastating. "What if I try and fail? I don't know if I can take the blow to my self-esteem." Most people experience some change anxiety as they grow. It's part of the process. When this change anxiety aligns itself with a fear of failure, it's overwhelming. A legitimate concern for outcomes is characteristic of high achievers. They weigh potential consequence rather than blindly seeking thrills. Help your salespeople understand change anxiety to avoid their confusing it with a fear of failing. Help them develop the necessary skills to ensure success.

A sixth and common reason why people remain in comfort zones is the fear of success. This manifests itself in three ways. One, high expectations. Time and again salespeople say, "Why should I push myself for the rest of this year and blow out my quota? They will expect me to do it again next year." The perception is that by working hard now the salesperson is setting himself up for the future. There's an ironic twist here. If you excel today and make it a habit then you will probably do it again tomorrow. Isn't that blasting out of a comfort zone? Those who fear the continued expectation of high effort seem to be haunted by their ambitions. They want to achieve but do not want to commit to a lifestyle of success.

Two, separation anxiety. When someone makes a decision to blast out of a comfort zone, she leaves others behind. It's a fear of being different or a fear of not belonging. Peers become subordinates. Old friends may not advance as quickly, which could produce tension. Family members may not fully accept the person's "new" behavior. A salesperson confided in me one day that she had considerable difficulty adjusting to her new role in life after achieving real sales success. She equated it to going off to kindergarten again. She felt that she was leaving people behind with every step ahead she took. The greater her success, the greater the distance from her past. Eventually, it overwhelmed her. She job hops now, always flirting with success but never embracing it as a lifestyle.

Three, "I don't deserve it!" No one really says this, but they think it, at least unconsciously. A major business publication ran a cover story about top executives and their fears of success. Seventy percent of those at the top expressed some reservations about their "deservability" during their climb to the top.

Let's try a sentence completion. Things are going well in your life. In fact, they couldn't be better. You recently got a promotion at work and are earning more money than you thought you would ever make. Your spouse also got a promotion. Your combined income is beyond your wildest dreams. You're playing three strokes below your golf handicap. Your tennis game has never been better. Your family life is incredible. Your children have won scholarships to college. You're elected president of a social group to which you belong. With all this great stuff happening in your life, you say to yourself . . .? How did you answer? Something bad is about to happen? In every group I do this with, including management groups, I hear a chorus of, "Something bad is around the corner. It just doesn't get that good for me." And they're right . . . at least in their own minds. We don't always get what we want but we always get what we expect.

When people feel this way, they sabotage themselves in not-so-subtle ways. I worked with a VP of sales who earned well into six figures his last year in sales. He confided in me that whenever he got too successful he buried his nose in a bag of cocaine or tried to drink a whiskey bottle dry. His success scared the living daylights out of him. Another salesperson I know job jumps every six months after she discovers how good she really is. Another salesperson I know quit a very lucrative sales career because he couldn't handle the guilt of earning more money in six months than his father earned in any three-year period as a laborer.

Others sabotage themselves more subtly. They miss appointments, fail to return phone calls to customers, forget literature, show up late for sales meetings, miss pages in proposals, etc. All of these keep them in comfort zones. It reminds me of my children watching a horror movie. They cover their eyes with their hands and peer between their fingers. At the scary parts they close their fingers, blocking their view. Many who fear success do this. They flirt with the notion, and when they get too close they cover their eyes, blocking the view. For whatever reason, they feel unworthy of success. If people can believe that life can't be that good, why can't they believe that it *can* be that good?

BLASTING OUT OF COMFORT ZONES

Teaching your salespeople to blast out of comfort zones is simple. Helping them get out of a comfort zone is more challenging. They need understanding, empathy, and encouragement. Most of all, they need a strategy and tactics that help them achieve this goal. Ideally, this strategy will help them gain control, understand the nuances of personal change, set progressively higher goals, take action, and celebrate their successes.

Step One: Seizing Control

Few things discourage people more than feeling out of control or not in control. On the other hand, being in control is energizing. The first step in helping your salespeople blast out of comfort zones is to teach them that they do have control over their destinies. They are not victims in their environments. Psychologists have long recognized this phenomenon and introduced a concept to explain it: *locus of control.* Locus (or location) refers to a person's perception of control over his life—either within him or outside him. Internally controlled people feel autonomous, in control, and responsible for much of what happens to them. Externally controlled people feel more vulnerable to outside forces. Fate controls their destinies. Externally controlled people feel that they have little if any influence over their personal outcomes. One sounds like the victim and the other the victor of their environments.

Internally controlled salespeople feel accountable for much of what happens in their territories. Reasonable people understand you can't control everything in your world. Internally controlled people accept that they wield significant power over their destinies—sales goals.

On the other hand, externally controlled salespeople feel less responsible for what happens in their territories—

good or bad. They perceive themselves as pawns in a business game of chess. When things go badly in their business, it's never their fault. Conversely, when things are great, they don't feel responsible for that either. They don't hear the inner applause.

Externally controlled salespeople send loud and clear messages for help. They say things like:

- "If I had your territory, I know I could do better."
- "You have all the luck. You get the best accounts."
- "It's not in the cards for me. I never get the breaks."
- "If we only had better literature, I could sell more."
- "I'm the new kid on the block. You can't sell when you're that new."
- "Our products aren't any good—that's why I can't sell."
- "You can't sell during tough economic times."
- "Why should I try hard? Just about the time I sell something, someone on the inside messes it up for me!"
- "It's not in my job description, I can't do it."
- "Women can't be successful in this industry."

In all these cases, you can hear the perceived helplessness in their voices. I actually heard a salesperson during a seminar break one day say to another salesperson, "If I had your phone extension, I know I could be just as successful as you." Imagine that! The one salesperson had discovered the magic—having the right phone extension. It's sad that the externally controlled salesperson truly believed it was the phone extension and not effort that made the difference.

Mastering one's destiny is not a genetic issue. People are not predisposed biologically one way or the other. We are not born with three thousand genes of internal and five thousand genes of external locus. These perceptions of control are shaped over the period of a lifetime by parents, teachers, coaches, peers, managers, and significant others in our lives. The good news is that what can be learned can be unlearned. People can be externally controlled on the job while being internally controlled at home. Sales managers can have a very positive impact on a salesperson's career by helping him accept reasonable and realistic control of his business life.

First, help your salespeople understand the difference between *choice* and *chance*. Chance means that you leave it to fate and luck. Choice means you decide. Implicit is control. Replaying selling scenarios in which the salesperson feels like the victim and focusing on his different choices illustrates his involvement in creating outcomes. While doing this, be empathic and supportive. Avoid anything that sounds accusatory. "What other options can you exercise?" is one way to *refocus his locus.*

Second, *planning.* Simple pencil-and-paper planning exercises help salespeople internalize their locus. When salespeople construct an account strategy on paper, they exercise positive control. They're saying, "This is what I want to happen when I call on this customer." Daily "Things-to-Do" lists with items the salesperson wants to accomplish focus him on how he chooses to use his time. Contrast this to the individual who comes into the office, grabs a cup of coffee, sits at her desk, and says, "OK, phone, ring. Tell me, world, what am I supposed to do today." Planning empowers your salesforce with confidence.

Third, *reframe.* A major issue of what you're dealing with is how they process information. Externally controlled salespeople view things through the prism of a helpless victim. Helping them reframe their perceptions more positively through the prism of an internally controlled person offers another perspective. When they begin to offer what appear to be externally controlled excuses for why they did not sell or do something, offer other possible explanations. Again, avoid the tendency to accuse or excuse them. A different perspective on why they lost the sale helps them understand their control over the sale. Use it as a learning experience.

Help them use more positive and internally control-ling language: *I won't* versus *I can't. When* versus *if. Choice* versus *chance. I will* versus *I wish.* When they receive com-pliments, encourage them to say "Thanks," not "It was nothing." When faced with potential obstacles, teach them to use the "if/then" question: "*If* something happens, *then* how will I maintain control?"

Salespeople are more likely to blast out of a comfort zone if they feel empowered: in control. Building this sense of control is a great way to build their confidence. When a salesperson feels in control, she naturally pursues addi-tional challenges with increased confidence. Small victo-ries build self-competence. The combined effect of building confidence and competence raises self-esteem. This em-powers her to tackle her environment head-on. As a man-ager, your role is significant to this process.

Step Two: Dream Big Dreams

Once you've helped your salespeople accept control for much of what happens in their professional lives, they're ready to dream big dreams. My children teach me a great deal about life. They constantly remind me that life is supposed to be fun and lived to its fullest.

Children are dreamers. Their vivid imaginations take them to places adults only read about. Children walk on the moon, sing at the Met, play professional sports, and perform world-class surgeries. They make mud pies, too. As crawlers, they dream of walking. As toddlers, they dream of running. They conceive of a world of possibilities for themselves. They take themselves to the edges of their imaginations.

When my oldest, Amanda, took her first steps, there

were no doubts in her mind that she was doing what her Creator had intended. She imagined herself walking just like Mom and Dad. At first, she inched her way along the coffee table in the living room, letting go momentarily, and standing on her own for a microsecond—just long enough to feel her weight completely supported by her legs. Then, she took a couple of steps and fell. She laughed. It was funny to her. "Hey, Mom and Dad, I fell. It's funny. I'm gonna try again." And she did. And she fell again. And she laughed again. For her, there was only one direction: forward. Today, she runs like a deer—just like in her dreams.

What happens to that "dreamability" in adults? Are we so stuffy that we no longer have time for such foolishness? Are we so busy with reality that fantasy is a luxury? Does the passage from adolescence to adulthood somehow sap from us the attitude or inclination to dream? When does it stop?

Blasting out of a comfort zone means dreaming of possibilities and potential. It's holding yourself to a higher standard of performance and saying, "I'm better than that." I bet that when you look back on those times in your life when you felt most alive and very close to becoming "more and more" of what you could become, you held yourself to a higher mental standard. You gave yourself permission to dream about what you could be. And you acted on that dream.

Robert Schuller has built a career helping people become possibility thinkers. For him it's a simple philosophy: "I would rather attempt a great many things in this world and fail than to attempt nothing and succeed."

What if we lived by "What if?" I've heard that the most expensive real estate in this country is not in Manhattan, but in cemeteries. There lies the hope of the future. The dreams that were never pursued. The buildings that were never built. The inventions never invented. The songs never composed. The novels never written. The cures never created. The dreams of those who failed to pursue them.

I was speaking in Keystone, Colorado, a couple of years ago and visited one of the tourist gift shops. I found a bumper sticker that read, "Don't Die Wondering!" Wow, what a message! I bought every one they had and plastered them throughout my office at home and at work. Aren't you the least bit curious what's inside you? I'm desperately curious about my potential. Potential is what we are capable of becoming. As you write the last chapter to your life, wouldn't it be a shame to discover that it's been a short story, not a *War and Peace*-length realization of your potential?

Teach your salespeople to raise the bar, hold themselves to higher standards, and dream about what they can become. Build their expectations while teaching them the skills to get there. Challenge them to think in terms of "What if?" What if I do that, sell that, read that, become that? Take them to the land of possibilities, encourage them to dream to the edges of their imaginations. . . .

Gandhi wrote, "Man often becomes what he believes himself to be. If I keep saying to myself that I cannot do a certain thing, it is possible that I may end life by becoming incapable of doing it. On the contrary, if I have the belief that I can do it, I shall surely acquire that capacity to do it even if I may not have it at the beginning." It's as if your ability will stretch to your capacity for believing.

Encourage your salespeople to dream about what they want from the job, the goals they want to achieve, and the path they want to take. Teach them to focus on these dreams with a laserlike intensity. Keep them on track with coaching and counseling. For them, blasting out of a comfort zone is learning to dream again and pursuing these dreams with wide-eyed enthusiasm. For the old dogs who are trying to learn new tricks, suggest that they may want to supplant cynicism with childlike naiveté. Children are often surprised by failure. Maybe it's because they do not expect it.

> *Dream lofty dreams, and as you dream, so shall you become. Your vision is the promise of what you shall one day be; your ideal is the prophecy of what you shall at last unveil.*
>
> James Allen

Step Three: Expect Buffeting

Change creates stress for many people. For some, it's positive. For others, it's negative. Earlier I described a zone around the comfort zone called the anxiety zone. It's the natural anxiety that accompanies moving toward one's potential—it's change.

In his first book, Chuck Yeager described what it was like to break the sound barrier. He said that at Mach 0.9 (the split second before breaking through the sound barrier) his airplane began to pitch, yaw, and buffet. It was some of the worst turbulence he had ever experienced. He felt the shock waves from the sound barrier. And then a curious thing happened. The moment he broke the sound barrier the buffeting stopped. It was some of the smoothest flying he had ever experienced.

What a great metaphor for what happens to people when they decide to blast out of a comfort zone. They experience the same type of buffeting. It's the pull to the familiar, the comfortable, the known. This is internal buffeting—what you feel on the inside. And because you're internally controlled you have a choice for how you would like to use this anxiety. It can be an inhibiting force that stifles and cripples you, or it can fuel your afterburner to propel you farther and faster. The choice belongs to you.

Change causes internal buffeting. It's part of the process. Somehow knowing that helps. Your left brain may say, "I understand it," but your right brain may say, "I still don't like it." Several years ago, I was scheduled to speak for six hours to seven hundred private practice physical therapists in Memphis at the Peabody Hotel. Prior to that, the largest group I addressed was seventy. That extra zero on the end may not sound like much to you, but to me it was intimidating—change anxiety.

I got up early that morning and by six o'clock I was onstage gasping at seven hundred empty chairs. I was scared. My knees rocked. My mouth went cotton-dry. And my head . . . I thought I would pass out. It startled me to think that I might feel this later in front of the group. I was really nervous. I went to a survival mode. I didn't even think about hitting a home run that day. I just didn't want to pass out onstage. Sound ridiculous? Not according to other speaker friends with whom I've talked over the years.

I convinced myself that I knew the material well enough to somehow muddle through the day. For reassurance, I replayed other intimidating experiences from different times in my life. I had experienced far worse things than standing in front of seven hundred excited people who really wanted me to succeed. It sounded good at the time. It worked.

Three hours later, as the program director read my introduction, I repeated silently, "Oh Lord, please don't let me pass out." The adrenaline rush was incredible. As I gingerly ran up the stairs and began my rehearsed opening, a curious thing happened. The extra shot of adrenaline ignited me with an unprecedented passion and exuberance. Two minutes later, I was off to the races! It was a great day. The audience loved the material and I loved them. My greatest fear evaporated into my greatest dream— my first standing ovation at the end of a presentation. That presentation still holds the record for highest tape sales in a single day!

This was an amazing life lesson for me. I was experiencing the natural buffeting that accompanies blasting out of a comfort zone. It taught me to positively anticipate it, welcome it, embrace it, use it, and benefit from it. Internal buffeting is a friend. It warns and energizes us. Trust it. It's part of the package for change. After fourteen hundred presentations, I still feel it to varying degrees. It's one signal that I'm alive and involved. You don't get that same rush by staying in a comfort zone.

Internal buffeting happens within us. External buffeting comes from those around us. When you decide to change things in your life, you affect others. And some go to great lengths to let you know they're uncomfortable with your new direction. You're slipping out of a role with which they feel very comfortable. In a way, you're taking them out of their comfort zones. As they experience some buffeting, they are kind enough to share it with you.

This is especially true for salespeople who try to sell new lines of products against a backdrop of cynicism from their peers. How many people attempt to climb out of their roles in life and face the discouragement of their friends and family? They hear things like, "Have you forgotten who you are and where you came from?" Some wear their pasts like shackles. Employees stretch to jeers of, "What are you doing? Bucking for a promotion?" Have you ever been on a diet and lost twenty pounds? It's not long before someone shoves a piece of chocolate cake in your face to let you know you're "looking ill."

This may sound horribly cynical. I don't mean it that way. My point is this: if you anticipate some external buffeting, you won't be blindsided by it. Anticipating doesn't mean it will happen or that you will create it. It simply means that being aware of the possibility prepares you to handle it better. The same is true for internal buffeting. Alerting yourself to this natural phenomenon enables you to use it to your advantage.

Advise your salespeople that as they attempt to blast

out of their comfort zones, buffeting is likely. Prepare them for it by discussing options for when it happens. What will they do when the pressure from within or outside gets too great? Will you be there to help them over the hump? What type of coping strategies will they use?

Step Four: Create Catalytic Events

At some point, your salespeople must break the inertia. These are catalytic events. They represent a change from *what was* to *what is*. It's important to start moving in the right direction. Often times, people create wonderful plans for change but are short on execution. They are always getting ready to get ready. Too much time goal-setting and not enough time goal-getting. Positive thinking without positive action is hopeful optimism at best. Get ready and get busy.

Catalytic events include things like a full day of cold calling, one day of dieting, demonstrating a new product line to customers, reading a book on financial planning, listening to motivational tapes, joining a professional association, or taking a course on assertiveness. It's any activity that represents positive action for stretching beyond a comfort zone. Get the momentum moving in the right direction.

Take baby steps to minimize the risk. Remember, your goal is to *get going*. Break the activities into small manageable units that minimize risk. For salespeople who don't cold call, a full month of it may be too overwhelming. Go for a day at a time.

Be sure to reinforce the effort or process of blasting out of a comfort zone. Nothing kills effort quicker than premature qualitative assessment. At first, trying is good enough. Your goal is to break inertia. Achieving production goals comes later.

Step Five: Celebrate Success

Replay success stories. Celebrate them. Recreate the event in your mind and the enthusiasm you felt. Put the fire back in your belly. Success is a great teacher. It gives you the mental and emotional information you need to duplicate it. As you replay the success, pay attention to the lesson and the feeling.

In a recent television interview, Ted Williams discussed his .406 batting average in 1941. The interviewer asked him what went through his mind during that season. Ted responded, "Every night when I went to bed I would lie awake for hours trying to figure out why that ball looked so big coming across the plate." His logic was simple. If he didn't know what he was doing right when he was doing it right, how could he do it right when he was doing it wrong? He learned from his success.

Most salespeople perform an autopsy on a sale that they lose. Few perform a postsale analysis for a piece of business they win. When your salespeople are on a roll, help them determine why. Celebrate the win. Use the emotion.

Winning is exciting. Achieving one's goals is rewarding. The emotional rush is a great energy to keep moving in the right direction. When your salespeople make significant efforts to blast out of their comfort zones, embellish the experience. Make it a big deal. Use the emotion to encourage future effort. Everyone needs a win now and again.

CHAPTER SUMMARY

Each of us experiences being in a comfort zone at some time in our lives. It's more of a "when" versus an "if" issue. At any given time, one out of four salespeople are stuck in a comfort zone. And there's no mystery about it. Everyone knows it, including the one who's stuck.

As a manager you can help your salespeople blast out of comfort zones by helping them gain control, encouraging them to dream, offering reassurance when they feel change anxiety, stressing action, and celebrating their efforts. Few things excite a manager more than helping someone reach beyond perceived limits and obstacles to become more and more of what he is capable of becoming. You are an important change agent.

9
Management Miscellany

This began as a chapter on management and leadership for sales managers. It grew quickly. The variety of issues sales managers face is as diverse as this chapter. In this chapter, salespeople describe their worst sales manager, I differentiate leadership styles, you learn how to use change to your advantage, manage in tough times, the role of value-added marketing, and how to involve distributors in value-added selling.

IN SEARCH OF PIT PERFORMANCE

Mark Twain observed something interesting about people and learning. He said that everyone can teach us something. To paraphrase him, the successful ones teach us what to do. And "God bless the failures in this world, for they teach us what *not* to do."

About the time people were writing books on peak performance and excellence, I thought it would be interesting to approach it from another angle. I asked salespeople in my seminars to describe their worst sales managers. The variety of answers to that question were curious. Six critical flaws of bad management surfaced. These turned into an article and aroused the interest of managers from around the country who wanted more information on what they could do to avoid the pitfalls of bad management practices.

The following list reads like "How to fail in management without really trying!" It's important to periodically review this checklist of "things *not* to do" and reframe them more positively.

Flaw Number One: Being Inconsistent

This includes a list of responses in which salespeople describe managers who "shirk responsibility, fail to practice what they preach, are incredibly disorganized, fail to demonstrate leadership qualities by being everyone's friend and nobody's bearer of tough news, shoot from the hip, and prematurely accuse people." Salespeople need managers who are fair and consistent.

Consistency builds trust. People need to know what to expect. Inconsistency and suspicion go hand in hand. When sales managers act inconsistently, salespeople tend to look over their shoulders and second-guess their own behavior. It's like the parent who says, "Do what I say not what I do."

Flaw Number Two: Being Unethical

One salesperson complained of a manager who accepted a job, cleaned house immediately, and replaced everyone with his cronies. Other things included "being secretive— almost clandestine, expecting salespeople to engage in questionable tactics to get new business, promising anything to get the business, and sneaking around like the FBI to check on employees." One salesperson described the sales manager who used to park his car at the end of the salesperson's street to determine what time the salesperson would leave every morning to make calls. Imagine getting a call from your neighbors alerting you that your boss was at it again. Embarrassing, isn't it?

Managers who behave in unethical ways communicate a strong message to salespeople that any behavior is justified as long as it creates the desired results. Is it any wonder that some salespeople promise a lot to customers and then fail to deliver? Whenever a sales manager asks me how to deal with salespeople who overpromise and underdeliver, I review what management has promised and failed to deliver. It doesn't take long for a lack of ethics at the top to make its way down to the rank and file.

Flaw Number Three: Not Communicating

The most common response I received was, "My boss never listens to me." Others included (my boss) "is out of touch with day-to-day operations," "is evasive when confronted with questions," "maintains poor eye contact," "fails to praise me or even acknowledge my accomplishments," "uses abusive language," or "criticizes me in public." When you look for what causes many relationships to turn sour, a breakdown in communications is at the very heart. Whether it's salespeople and managers, customers and suppliers, husbands and wives, children and parents, or friends who are out of sync, failing to communicate is the root cause.

Flaw Number Four: Intimidating

I broached this earlier in the section on reinforcement schedules. Punishment is a short-term motivator at best. It breeds compliance without commitment. You can "beat people into submission" and bully them with threats, but it destroys the individual's spirit of cooperation and contribution to organizational objectives. A greater concern is the lack of dignity and respect it shows the individual. Everyone deserves to be treated with respect.

The response that stands out most in my mind came from a salesperson who described "threat sessions" instead of sales meetings. He said that the sales manager would assemble the troops and proceed to "chew" on them for failing to meet goals. He never gave positive feedback on their performance and nothing was ever good enough for him. Rather than encouraging the salesforce and attempting to inspire them with positive feelings of self-worth, he intimidated and threatened them, which resulted in high turnover.

Flaw Number Five: Being Selfish

I found this group of responses especially interesting. When you cut through many of the specific responses, a key variable is the manager's insecurity or greed. Managers who fail to share key information with employees are really saying that they are afraid of what the employees may do with the information when they receive it. Being selfish also surfaced as not letting the employee grow at a pace that benefited the employee. The manager didn't feel comfortable with an employee who was on the fast track.

Another example was the manager who did not want to share responsibility with his salesforce and came across as very insecure, thinking the salesforce might try to "show him up." The most colorful example came from the salesperson who increased sales significantly and management failed to share the rewards. The salesperson felt that she gave a lot better than she got, left the company, opened a competing business, and gave her previous employer tough competition. All this happened because the sales manager failed to recognize and act on the perceived inequity.

Flaw Number Six: Not Directing

Specifically, salespeople complained of the manager's failure to train, provide instructions, or offer insight into problems. "They left me out there to sink or swim on my own" was typical of what I heard. Managers who believe in the "sink or swim" philosophy lose some great talent along the way. These managers rationalize their lack of direction by saying things like, "The cream will rise to the top," or "We give people the opportunity to succeed or fail." Even passive management support fails to give salespeople the substantial direction they need for success.

Focusing on results only, without emphasis on the methods, leaves salespeople confused about acceptable standards of performance. Newer salespeople need lots of time and attention from management. Research demonstrates that the salesperson's first manager is the most influential person in the rookie's career. It's then that the patterns for success or failure are set.

Imagine hiring someone for a dangerous and technically demanding job and not providing even rudimentary instruction for operating the equipment? It's a disaster waiting to happen. The same thing happens to salespeople, on a different level, when management fails to guide and direct them.

As a sales manager, a fundamental issue you must address is your management style when dealing with subordinates. You're either building them up or breaking them down. Scanning the following list helps you identify the best approach.

- Build *consistency* into your approach and system for salespeople.
- Establish *ethical* standards of performance and lead by example.
- *Communicate* with your salespeople: listen!
- *Encourage* your salespeople: build them up!

- *Share* the rewards—be lavish with praise and recognition.
- *Direct* them for success.

MANAGEMENT AND LEADERSHIP

Is there a difference? Yes. You can manage without leading, you can lead without managing, you can lead and manage, and you can do neither.

Management is directing, supervising, controlling, or administering. Managers achieve organizational objectives with available resources. Sales managers are responsible for the day-to-day operation of the salesforce. *Leadership* is empowering others, guiding, influencing, directing, and setting the tone. Leaders are visionary. It is possible and desirable for sales managers to be both to their salesforce. They must both manage and lead their people.

Too much management and not enough leadership sounds a great deal like an administrator. Leading without managing at the field sales level fails to provide the direct supervisory feedback salespeople need. Research supports that strong leaders share these characteristics:

- They have a strong commitment to the job.
- They involve employees.
- They are goal-oriented versus procedures-oriented.
- They communicate openly with their subordinates.
- They share their vision and give concrete instructions for achieving it.
- They balance their task orientation with empathy for others.

There are many different leadership styles. Think of the most effective leader for whom you've worked. What characterized his or her approach? Did the approach change to fit the nuances of each management scenario? Your management and leadership style generally fits into one of several categories and may even shift depending on situational variables.

Micromanagement and Macromanagement

Micromanagers are more detail-oriented. They focus on procedures, methods, and processes. Their major concern is efficiency and expediency. Their management approach is more direct and supervisory. Is this style ever appropriate? When you manage a rookie salesperson who doesn't have a clue about his job and needs very careful overseeing, this style makes tremendous sense. Also, employees who struggle may need a micromanager.

On the other hand, macromanagers tend to look at the big picture instead of details. They are more results-oriented than procedures-oriented. If efficiency is the watchword for the micromanager, then effectiveness is the watchword for the macromanager. They are more likely to guide than supervise. Micromanagers may *delegate and do* while macromanagers *delegate and monitor*.

So which is appropriate for you? It depends on the complexity of the job, the talents and abilities of your staff, and the culture in which they work: i.e., your situation. It makes sense to macromanage a successful and experienced salesperson. Too much direct supervision will stifle and smother him. Your challenge is to ensure that you are situationally appropriate.

Theory X and Theory Y Management

Over thirty years ago, Douglas McGregor wrote *The Human Side of Enterprise*. This heralded the birth of the human relations movement in management and the demise of scientific management, which dominated the scene for fifty years in America.

The prescriptions of the human relations movement sound as contemporary today as they did revolutionary in 1960. Involve employees in management decisions. Challenge workers by redesigning jobs that encourage participation. Open the communication channels between managers and subordinates. How could anyone argue with such commonsense psychology?

McGregor described two sets of assumptions under which managers operate. The first he called Theory X management and the other he called Theory Y management. This brief summary of the two different styles may help you understand some of your biases.

Theory X managers believe people dislike work so much that they will try to avoid it; direct coercion, threats, and punishment are the only ways to move people into achieving organizational objectives; and most people have little ambition and avoid responsibility.

Theory X sales managers think like this:

- Money is the only motivator salespeople need.
- Most salespeople are lazy and will slough off given the chance.
- Most salespeople need a kick in the backside to get moving.
- Salespeople sell only the easiest products and will take the path of least resistance.

Theory Y managers believe that expending effort at work is natural; punishment and threats are not the only ways to get people moving; people will commit to organization objectives; employees will seek responsibility in the right environment; and most people have the intellect and drive to do great work.

Theory Y sales managers think like this:

- My people respond well to the opportunity for personal growth.

- Job enrichment, challenge, and creative expression are powerful motivators for salespeople.
- Our system probably underutilizes the talents of our people.
- Given the chance and right management climate, our people will seek additional responsibility.

Most sales managers I've trained test as Theory Y. Intellectually, they understand the approach and fancy themselves as the more positive and progressive manager. Living the Theory Y management style is more challenging. I witness many Theory X management behaviors from people who perceive themselves differently.

Many people confuse micromanaging with Theory X. Their perception is that closely directing an employee is Theory X. I can't think of one scenario in which Theory X management assumptions are correct. I can conceive of many scenarios in which a more directed management approach is appropriate. To demonstrate Theory X behaviors, you must believe that people are lazy and must be coerced. How could anything positive result from that?

In management, we pretty much get back that which we look for. If we look for lazy, we find it. If we look for responsibility-shirking employees, they too appear. If we look for challenge-driven, opportunity-seeking, self-motivating, growth-oriented salespeople, they are there. Employees mirror your expectations.

Task Versus People Orientation

This is the yin and yang of management psychology. For decades, researchers have explored the issue of task versus people orientation to describe the ideal leadership model. The labels they've used for task include: boss-centered, autocratic, directive, initiating structure, results-oriented, and Theory X. People labels include: empathy, democratic, employee-centered, supportive, and Theory Y. The primary concern of these researchers has been to identify what works best: high-task/high-people; high-task/low-people; or low-task/high-people.

Results are mixed. A task-oriented environment may get the results you want at the expense of job satisfaction and turnover and absenteeism. On the other hand, a people-oriented environment may foster lower absenteeism and higher job satisfaction, but the results suffer. There must be some middle ground.

Extracting the best from both climates makes the most sense. Sales managers who recognize the importance of achieving organizational objectives with and through their salespeople have a distinct advantage over those sales managers who attempt to reach numerical quotas in spite of their people. Using the "best of both worlds" approach seems both reasonable and achievable. At times, you may shift from a more people-oriented environment to a task-driven environment to meet deadlines. The reverse is also true. Coming off a particularly difficult assignment and high-pressure deadlines, you are well advised to pay attention to the people issues.

Reacting and proacting to whichever is situationally appropriate is the hallmark of the effective sales manager. Knowing when to attend to the task and when to attend to your people gives you a decided edge. Moving your group toward organizational objectives while remaining sensitive to their needs is fundamental to your success. Assessing each person's priority is your critical intuitive skill.

MANAGERS AS CHANGE AGENTS

Changing your environment to a value-added sales culture is what this book is all about. To facilitate this change it's important to understand how people and organizations change.

Does your organization need to change? This type of cultural assessment question is a great place to start. *Do you have a product-driven or market-driven culture?* Market-driven cultures are far more amenable to value-added selling. If your company dictates value-added to the customer, then your cultural problems run deeper than the scope of this book. *Does your culture support a value-added selling philosophy?* This last question includes products, people, and systems. It's difficult for your salespeople to sell value-added if your products are inferior, service lacking, and systems antiquated. Perhaps the most important question to ask is . . . *Do you offer value-added?*

Organizational Change

Organizations, like people, go through a change process. Understanding the process and your role in it empowers you as the primary change agent. Your credibility with the group coupled with their understanding and accepting the urgency of change expedite the process.

Prior to implementing change, some *tension* (internal or external) drives the process. Tension can be anything that creates awareness, understanding, and acceptance that change must happen. This includes increased competitive pressures, customer complaints, lower profit margins, management admonishments about a diminished market position, salesforce warnings of service gaps, or eroding financial stability.

During this phase the organization *thaws*. Cultural paradigms frozen solid from years of inertia begin to melt in the heat of tension. Management intervenes with change strategies designed to rescue the organization from a certain slow death of attrition. Smart managers try to make the MOST of change:

- Mission—they establish and agree on the company's mission: the vision.

- Objectives—they set objectives to support the mission: the goals.
- Strategy—they outline a strategy for achieving the objectives: the "what" to do.
- Tactics—they detail the tactics that support the strategy: the "how" to do it.

There are a number of change dynamics that facilitate the process. First, your understanding and acknowledging the natural resistance that accompanies change helps build your credibility and trust with employees. The reality is that change scares the pants off most of them.

Second, change is easier when it's a top-down process. You must "buy into" the concept and convince employees that everyone has the same priority. Otherwise, employees feed back the lip service you've paid.

Third, change begins conceptually with an idea and eventually filters into field-level tactics that bring about the change. Your direct involvement is higher at the conceptual level and the employee's involvement is higher at the tactical level. Involvement lowers resistance to change. The earlier you involve employees the quicker they "buy into" the process. Make them part of the change process—not just pawns in the game.

Fourth, open communication increases the likelihood that change will happen. You must be accessible to employees during this critical phase. Share your vision for the future, communicate the urgency for change, and impassion employees with your enthusiasm.

As the paradigms melt away, change is applied and monitored. Once in place, you must reinforce it. Solidify it. Ingrain it. Imprint it. Reward it. Make it stick.

How People Change

When I first got into the sales training business, I spent a great deal of time researching change and why people resist it. Eleven years later it still fascinates me. The customer who says, "We're happy with our current supplier," the salesperson who resists training by saying, "We sell differently in our market," and the manager who reacts with, "Our business is different," are all clinging to the familiar, the known, and the predictable.

Implementing a value-added sales campaign is change. It's unrealistic to expect that your salespeople will not resist it. Understanding where they are with the change and what they are feeling helps you expedite the process and build commitment. The Change Process Matrix™ diagram (Figure 10) explains where your people are and your role.

FIGURE 10
CHANGE PROCESS MATRIX™

HOW PEOPLE CHANGE

	I	II	III	IV
Phase	Status Quo	Understanding	Acceptance	Action
Buy-In: Intellectual Emotional	No No	Yes No	Yes Yes	Yes Yes
Reaction and Motivators	Denial (avoidance)	Clinging (security)	Longing	Excitement
Your Task	Raise the constructive internal "pain level"	Empathize and educate	Plan and reassure	Monitor and reinforce

In phase one, people want to maintain the status quo. They do not want change. Their primary motivator is homeostasis. They're in a comfort zone! They actively avoid and deny change. As a change agent, your task is to raise the "constructive pain level" so that they understand the urgency (the tension) to change. You can do this by explaining to them the consequences of action versus inertia. Help them feel the tension to change. And, you should expect that they will defend against this. It's a natural part of the process. Helping them understand the necessity for change is superior to dictating change and forcing compliance without commitment. Sell them on the need to change, just as if they were customers.

In phase two, people understand intellectually that they may need to change but emotionally they reject it. In fact, they cling to the old way of doing things. Their security boats are rocking and they don't like it. Demonstrate empathy and understanding. Continue to educate them on the need to change and promise a better future. The battleship is turning. Don't quit now.

Phase three brings intellectual and emotional acceptance of the inevitable change. People still long for the old ways but recognize and accept the importance of moving forward. They have "bought in," and your job is to keep the momentum going. Share plans. Discuss tactics. Offer reassurance.

Phase four is exciting. Everyone is on the bandwagon and optimistic about the future. The plan has become action. Employees support it. There's plenty of positive emotion. Keep things moving positively and "freeze" the commitment into the cultural paradigm. The new way becomes the standard for the future. Value-added selling becomes the dominant sales philosophy. You've created significant change.

MANAGING IN TOUGH TIMES

One reason you bought this book is that you're probably feeling some pressure from tough economic conditions in your industry or you're trying to avert tough times. It's a relevant topic for all of us. Prior to the current economic slowdown, we spent three years studying what companies do in tough times to thrive not just survive. We scanned articles, listened to the pundits, suffered through research data, and talked to those in the trenches. Here's what we discovered.

During tough times . . .

- 5% of all companies will thrive.
- 25% will fail.
- 70% will just survive.

The good news is that you've got a choice. You can determine which category is for you: a thriver, a survivor, or one who failed. How you conduct business in tough times determines this for you.

Salespeople Mistakes

We discussed the three biggest mistakes salespeople make during tough times. One, they choose to cut price instead of add value. They prefer to cut price instead of holding the line and trying to sell the customer on the value-added package. Salespeople are scared and cave in to competitive and customer pressures. The really bad news is that those profit margins do not rebound. Price cutting destroys the integrity of the sales price. Once the price goes down, it stays down.

Two, they reduce face-to-face calling by 38 percent. They call at 62 percent the calling rate of good economic times. This paradox was revealed by the Purchasing Management Association. For whatever reasons—attempting to control sales expenses, discouragement, or reduction in forces—company representatives fail to get the coverage in tough times they get in good times. This was the most difficult for us to understand and accept.

Three, salespeople believe everything their customers tell them and allow it to bias their presentations. If a salesperson hears several price objections in one day, he naturally expects more from the rest of his customer base. Salespeople lead with, "I guess things are as tough for you as they are for everyone else?" Sharp customers hear desperation in the salesperson's voice and hold the line on pricing a bit longer when negotiating.

Manager Mistakes

Managers also make their share of mistakes during tough times. First, they believe everything salespeople tell them. They fail to get into the field and verify these things first-hand. It leaves them vulnerable and uninformed. They implement strategies based on conjecture.

Second, they engage in radical slashing of expenses instead of prudent pruning. Across-the-board cuts slash away at budgets like advertising and marketing. In tough times, the marketing noise level is much lower than in good times. The return on investment is much higher. Some people estimate you get two and a half times the bang for your buck. Yet managers miss this opportunity by overreacting to the economy.

Third, they fail to have a plan in place for tough times. Consequently, they react out of panic. How prudent can your decisions be when you're acting on news from the field and the media telling you how tough things are?

Prescriptions

Salespeople need to sell value instead of price. Hold the line on discounting. Reinforce the value-added benefits of your company. Encourage your salespeople to increase the direct face-to-face calling by 25 percent. This, in effect, doubles your coverage relative to the competition. Train your salespeople to selectively input what they hear from the media and the marketplace. Some industries are experiencing explosive growth, but we never hear about them.

Take everything your salespeople say with a grain of salt. Visit the field more to confirm what you hear. Reassure customers that your company is doing fine and will be a player for a long time to come. Take with you a message of optimism. Your voice may be the only positive thing the field will hear. Prudently trim expenses in those areas that contain the most fat. To determine that, go to the source— employees. Ask them where the waste is. They should know—they work with it. And mostly, leave your advertising budget alone. Capitalize on the market conditions to get a greater return on your advertising dollars.

You've got a choice on where you want your company to be at the end of the tough times you're experiencing. Use it as a time to get lean and mean. Regroup and redeploy. Many see it as a type of corporate cleansing. It will get better. It always does.

All things are difficult before they are easy.
Robert Fuller

VALUE-ADDED MARKETING

My seminar has never been a marketing program, yet some of my strongest proponents come from marketing departments. This is a book for sales managers, yet I anticipate directors of marketing will use it to support their groups.

Value marketing has become fashionable. Advertisers use the word *value* in their ads to convince consumers that they offer the best deal. National magazines run cover stories on the concept. It's as if the decade of the nineties will be ten years of educated consumers looking for the best overall buy for their dollar. So how does marketing support the salesforce in selling value-added?

First, they provide salespeople with the market intelligence that they need to play tough, competitive hardball.

Direct comparative selling is accepted in today's marketplace. Value-added salespeople must have at their fingertips in-depth knowledge about the competition to beat them. Would you go into battle without enemy intelligence? Additionally, knowledge about the marketplace and industry trends builds the salesforce's mental capital.

What type of support materials has your marketing department developed? Literature extolling your value-added? Testimonial letter brochures that brag about your total package of services? Value In Purchasing lists? Question books that help buyers make better long-term decisions? Competitive analysis reports for dealers and consumers?

How does your advertising support the value-added theme? Are you using the terminology "value-added" in the ads to position your company as *the* value-added resource? Or does your advertising support a price-buyer mindset? Do your ads address the bundled package concept or only promote products? Does your marketing department use PR such as well-written articles about your company in prestigious trade journals? Do they turn these into mailers for target markets? And the list goes on.

Perhaps the bigger question is, "How do sales and marketing in our company work together to create a value-added strategy?" Are you in sync? Can you have the salesforce selling price and the marketing department emphasizing value-added? Is there a coordinated push/pull program? Serious players work as a team.

I define marketing in much broader terms than most people do. It's all those activities in which you engage to attract, sell, distribute, and service your customers. It's the condition of your delivery trucks, the attitudes of your drivers, the tone of your receptionist's voice, the cleanliness of your office, the modernization of your facilities, the correspondence that goes out on your letterhead, the packaging of your product, how clean your salespeople keep their company cars, the bureaucracy of your system, your environmental impact, your community spirit, and your attitude toward employees. Every one of these things communicates something to someone about your company. Isn't that marketing?

DISTRIBUTORS ADDING VALUE

Are you adding value or cost? That question spawned a series of articles I wrote for distributors. For many, it's a painful question to answer. Having been on both sides of the issue, manufacturing and distribution, I understand the distributor's role and the supplier's dilemma.

Manufacturers complain that distributor salespeople are order-takers burdened by too many lines. They complain that distributors will drop the price at the slightest hint of price resistance and then come back to the supplier for a better deal to help absorb the loss. "Distributors are cutting back on inventory levels," manufacturers cry.

Distributors complain of diminished loyalty by vendors. "They don't care about us anymore—they won't hesitate to go direct." Distributors perceive manufacturers as having unreasonable ordering policies. "The manufacturers have cut back on training and development for our people." Each has a favorite ax to grind with the other.

The point is that distributors can add significant value and manufacturers are well-advised to work with their distributors to create a bigger bundled package of services. Give your distributor reps the product training they need to compete. Help them focus more strategically on key target accounts: Jumbo CD prospects. Work with them to overcome the mindset that 30 percent of nothing is better than 10 percent of something. Help them to become more proactive in selling value over price. Joint call often. Monopolize their time so they can't sell other lines.

Send monthly joint-call reports "tangiblizing" the business you're helping them develop. Work with their inside people to build a loyalty to your brand. Send business their way. Avoid going direct if at all possible. Instead, offer the distributor some other concession to compensate them for taking it on the chin with selling price. Train them on the skills presented in this book—teach them to be value-added sellers.

Encourage them to develop their own VIP list, Critical Buying Path, bundled package of services, and responses to price objections. Share your knowledge and enthusiasm. Teach them to evaluate things from the customer's perspective: value received versus value-added. It benefits no one to complain of each other's performance. Concentrate on fixing the problem instead of fixing the blame. It benefits both of you to work together. Consolidate your energy in a full-thrust attack on your competition.

CHAPTER SUMMARY

You purchased this book to make changes in your organization. It takes a strong leader to walk point on this operation. Managers supervise and leaders lead. You must be both. As you implement this change creating a value-added sales culture, remain sensitive to what your group is feeling. They're concerned. They, too, want what's best for the company. They may have trouble articulating it. Your job is to help redirect their focus.

Your marketing department would love an opportunity to augment your value-added selling efforts. Give them the chance. Develop a coordinated strategy. And work with your distributors. They need your leadership. Many do not have your resources. Remember, you will get back that which you look for in others.

10
Where Now . . .
And What Next?

"Where do I go from here and what do I do next?" Legitimate and reasonable questions. You purchased this book because something caught your attention. It attracted you because there was and probably still is some "tension" in your sales culture. Something is crying for change.

Changing requires planning, action, and persistence. The first half of this book introduced you to the concept of value-added selling. The second half focused on key management issues. The first half gave you the foundation knowledge to share with your salesforce and the second half the management skills to make it happen.

We've all heard the action clichés:

A journey of a thousand miles begins with a single step.

Ready, aim, fire!

The only way to start is to start.

To begin, begin.

Well begun is half done.

A good beginning cometh a good end.

188

And the list goes on. One of my favorites is, "There is no heavier burden than a great opportunity." Depending on your perspective at this point, you either have a great opportunity point or a tremendous burden.

In the appendix, I've included some practice exercises for you to use with your group. It will assist you in your efforts to implement a value-added sales culture. Use these exercises. Introduce your staff to the concept. Sell them on the urgency of doing this. Ignite them with your passion for a philosophy of maximum performance—not minimum standards. Help them, your company, and yourself become all that you can become!

Happy value-added selling! And God bless!

Appendix:
Practice Exercises

Awaken your group to the need for selling value . . . not price! Educate them on the "tension" your company feels to change. Share this book with your employees. Have them read the first half of it to familiarize themselves with the concept of value-added selling. Use these ideas in presenting the techniques to your staff. Call with them, give them performance feedback, and guide them on how to adjust to the new skills. Then go back and call some more with them. The amount of blood, sweat, and tears you personally put into this campaign will multiply exponentially by your number of salespeople.

Exercise Number One: Creating Tension

In this session, introduce the terms: value, value-added, and value-added selling. Discuss the conditions that drive your industry now. Elaborate on the pressures your company feels to respond and how the value-added advantage is the best option. Reinforce your point with the statistics on price shoppers and what customers really want. Your objective is to sell the group on the need and the solution.

Exercise Number Two: Build Their Knowledge Base

You want to prepare your group for selling value-added. They need information about the market, the competition, your company, and the customer. The questions from the strategic value analysis in Chapter 2 help you guide this discussion. You may even want to prepare a list of these in advance of your training session for the group to consider and answer.

Exercise Number Three: The Customer Audit

When your staff begins to view your value-added as value received, they have made the transition to value-added sellers. You can facilitate this change by concentrating on the customer's perception of value. Discuss the importance of probing and have them design a list of the twenty most important questions they can ask to draw out the customer's enhanced needs. Explain the concept of the Critical Buying Path and how they can use it to view life from the customer's perspective.

Exercise Number Four: The Bundled Presentation

A fundamental selling skill value-added salespeople use is presenting the bundled package solution. In Chapter 2, I discussed this concept and how your people can plan and present it. Teach them to infuse their sales vocabulary with enhancement tips like analogies, financial-justification examples, and value-added sales jargon. Prepare them to answer the question, "Why should I pay more to do business with your company?" The spontaneity with which they respond broadcasts a confidence and conviction that reassures buyers.

Exercise Number Five: Price Resistance

Luck is where preparation meets opportunity. When your salespeople have prepared responses to price objections and meet the opportunity to share this with buyers, they get real lucky. Introduce them to the three-step model. Elaborate on the many response strategies in Chapter 4. Have them role-play these tough customer scenarios. Build their confidence.

Exercise Number Six: Customer Service

Defensive selling is one of the most important advances in my field. Get that message to your staff. Explain how their role changes after the sale. They become customer-satisfaction specialists and growth specialists. Help them understand the relationship between performance and expectations. Empower them to serve and make decisions that affect customers. Teach them to accept the ultimate reality that everyone is responsible for customer satisfaction.

For more information on Tom Reilly and his seminars, cassette packages, and other books, contact:

> Sales Motivational Services
> 171 Chesterfield Industrial Boulevard
> Chesterfield, Missouri 63005-1219
> (314) 537-3360